Scarborough, and The Critic

Richard Brinsley Sheridan

A Trip to Scarborough

A COMEDY

DRAMATIS PERSONA

AS ORIGINALLY ACTED AT DRURY LANE THEATRE IN 1777

LORD FOPPINGTON *Mr. Dodd.*

SIR TUNBELLY CLUMSY *Mr. Moody.*

COLONEL TOWNLY *Mr. Brereton.*

LOVELESS *Mr. Smith.*

TOM FASHION *Mr. J. Palmer.*

LA VAROLE *Mr. Burton.*

LORY *Mr. Baddeley.*

PROBE *Mr. Parsons.*

MENDLEGS *Mr. Norris.*

JEWELLER *Mr. Lamash*

SHOEMAKER *Mr. Carpenter.*

TAILOR *Mr. Parker.*

AMANDA *Mrs. Robinson.*

BERINTHIA *Miss Farren.*

MISS HOYDEN *Mrs. Abington.*

MRS. COUPLER *Mrs. Booth.*

NURSE *Mrs. Bradshaw.*

Sempstress, Postilion, Maid, *and* Servants.

SCENE—SCARBOROUGH AND ITS NEIGHBOURHOOD.

PROLOGUE
SPOKEN BY MR. KING

What various transformations we remark,
From east Whitechapel to the west Hyde Park!
Men, women, children, houses, signs, and fashions,
State, stage, trade, taste, the humours and the passions;
The Exchange, 'Change Alley, wheresoe'er you're ranging,
Court, city, country, all are changed or changing
The streets, some time ago, were paved with stones,
Which, aided by a hackney-coach, half broke your bones.
The purest lovers then indulged in bliss;
They ran great hazard if they stole a kiss.
One chaste salute! —the damsel cried—Oh, fie!
As they approach'd—slap went the coach awry—
Poor Sylvia got a bump, and Damon a black eye.

But now weak nerves in hackney-coaches roam,
And the cramm'd glutton snores, unjolted, home;
Of former times, that polish'd thing a beau,
Is metamorphosed now from top to toe;
Then the full flaxen wig, spread o'er the shoulders,
Conceal'd the shallow head from the beholders.
But now the whole's reversed—each fop appears,
Cropp'd and trimm'd up, exposing head and ears:
The buckle then its modest limits knew,
Now, like the ocean, dreadful to the view,
Hath broke its bounds, and swallowed up the shoe:
The wearer's foot like his once fine estate,
Is almost lost, the encumbrance is so great.
Ladies may smile—are they not in the plot?
The bounds of nature have not they forgot?
Were they design'd to be, when put together,
Made up, like shuttlecocks, of cork and feather?
Their pale-faced grandmammas appeared with grace
When dawning blushes rose upon the face;
No blushes now their once-loved station seek;
The foe is in possession of the cheek!
No heads of old, too high in feather'd state,
Hinder'd the fair to pass the lowest gate;
A church to enter now, they must be bent,
If ever they should try the experiment.

As change thus circulates throughout the nation,
Some plays may justly call for alteration;
At least to draw some slender covering o'er,
That *graceless wit*[Footnote: "And *Van* wants grace, who never
    wanted wit. "—POPE.]which was too bare before:
Those writers well and wisely use their pens,
Who turn our wantons into Magdalens;
And howsoever wicked wits revile 'em,
We hope to find in you their stage asylum.

ACT I.

SCENE I. — *The Hall of an Inn.*

Enter TOM FASHION and LORY, POSTILION following with a portmanteau.

Fash. Lory, pay the postboy, and take the portmanteau.

Lory. [Aside to TOM FASHION.] Faith, sir, we had better

let the postboy take the portmanteau and pay himself.

Fash. [Aside to LORY.] Why, sure, there's something left in it!

Lory. Not a rag, upon my honour, sir! We eat the last of

your wardrobe at New Malton—and, if we had had twenty miles

further to go, our next meal must have been of the cloak-bag.

Fash. Why, 'sdeath, it appears full!

Lory. Yes, sir—I made bold to stuff it with hay, to save appearances, and look like baggage.

Fash. [Aside.] What the devil shall I do? —[*Aloud.*]

Hark'ee, boy, what's the chaise?

Post. Thirteen shillings, please your honour.

Fash. Can you give me change for a guinea?

Post. Oh, yes, sir.

Lory. [Aside.] So, what will he do now? —[*Aloud.*]

Lord, sir, you had better let the boy be paid below.

1

Fash. Why, as you say, Lory, I believe it will be as well.

Lory. Yes, yes, I'll tell them to discharge you below, honest friend.

Post. Please your honour, there are the turnpikes too.

Fash. Ay, ay, the turnpikes by all means.

Post. And I hope your honour will order me something for myself.

Fash. To be sure; bid them give you a crown.

Lory. Yes, yes—my master doesn't care what you charge them—so get along, you—

Post. And there's the ostler, your honour.

Lory. Psha! damn the ostler! —would you impose upon the

gentleman's generosity? —[*Pushes him out.*] A rascal, to be so cursed ready with his change!

Fash. Why, faith, Lory, he had nearly posed me.

Lory. Well, sir, we are arrived at Scarborough, not worth a guinea! I hope you'll own yourself a happy man—you have outlived all your cares.

Fash. How so, sir?

Lory. Why, you have nothing left to take care of.

Fash. Yes, sirrah, I have myself and you to take care of still.

Lory. Sir, if you could prevail with somebody else to do that for you, I fancy we might both fare the better for it. But now, sir, for my Lord Foppington, your elder brother.

Fash. Damn my eldest brother.

Lory. With all my heart; but get him to redeem your annuity, however. Look you, sir; you must wheedle him, or you must starve.

Fash. Look you, sir; I would neither wheedle him, nor starve.

Lory. Why, what will you do, then?

Fash. Cut his throat, or get someone to do it for me.

Lory. Gad so, sir, I'm glad to find I was not so well acquainted with the strength of your conscience as with the weakness of your purse.

Fash. Why, art thou so impenetrable a blockhead as to believe he'll help me with a farthing?

Lory. Not if you treat him *de haut en bas*, as you used to do.

Fash. Why, how wouldst have me treat him?

Lory. Like a trout—tickle him.

Fash. I can't flatter.

Lory. Can you starve?

Fash. Yes.

Lory. I can't. Good by t'ye, sir.

Fash. Stay—thou'lt distract me. But who comes here? My old friend, Colonel Townly.

Enter COLONEL TOWNLY.

My dear Colonel, I am rejoiced to meet you here.

Col. Town. Dear Tom, this is an unexpected pleasure! What, are you come to Scarborough to be present at your brother's wedding?

Lory. Ah, sir, if it had been his funeral, we should have come with pleasure.

Col. Town. What, honest Lory, are you with your master still?

Lory. Yes, sir; I have been starving with him ever since I saw your honour last.

Fash. Why, Lory is an attached rogue; there's no getting rid of him.

Lory. True, sir, as my master says, there's no seducing me from his service. —[*Aside*.] Till he's able to pay me my wages.

Fash. Go, go, sir, and take care of the baggage.

Lory. Yes, sir, the baggage! —O Lord! [*Takes up the portmanteau*.] I suppose, sir, I must charge the landlord to be very particular where he stows this?

Fash. Get along, you rascal. —[*Exit* LORY *with the portmanteau*.] But, Colonel, are you acquainted with my proposed sister-in-law?

Col. Town. Only by character. Her father, Sir Tunbelly Clumsy, lives within a quarter of a mile of this place, in a lonely old house, which nobody comes near. She never goes abroad, nor sees company at home; to prevent all misfortunes, she has her breeding within doors; the parson of the parish teaches her to play upon the dulcimer, the clerk to sing, her nurse to dress, and her father to dance; —in short, nobody has free admission there but our old acquaintance, Mother Coupler, who has procured your brother this match, and is, I believe, a distant relation of Sir Tunbelly's.

Fash. But is her fortune so considerable?

Col. Town. Three thousand a year, and a good sum of money, independent of her father, beside.

Fash. 'Sdeath! that my old acquaintance, Dame Coupler, could not have thought of me, as well as my brother, for such a prize.

Col. Town. Egad, I wouldn't swear that you are too late— his lordship, I know, hasn't yet seen the lady—and, I believe, has quarrelled with his patroness.

Fash. My dear Colonel, what an idea have you started!

Col. Town. Pursue it, if you can, and I promise you shall have my assistance; for, besides my natural contempt for his lordship, I have at present the enmity of a rival towards him.

Fash. What, has he been addressing your old flame, the widow Berinthia?

Col. Town. Faith, Tom, I am at present most whimsically circumstanced. I came here a month ago to meet the lady you mention; but she failing in her promise, I, partly from pique and partly from idleness, have been diverting my chagrin by offering up incense to the beauties of Amanda, our friend Loveless's wife. *Fash.* I never have seen her, but have heard her spoken of as a youthful wonder of beauty and prudence.

Col. Town. She is so indeed; and, Loveless being too careless and insensible of the treasure he possesses, my lodging in the same house has given me a thousand opportunities of making my assiduities acceptable; so that, in less than a fortnight, I began to bear my disappointment from the widow with the most Christian resignation.

Fash. And Berinthia has never appeared?

Col. Town. Oh, there's the perplexity! for, just as I began not to care whether I ever saw her again or not, last night she arrived.

Fash. And instantly resumed her empire.

Col. Town. No, faith—we met—but, the lady not condescending to give me any serious reasons for having fooled me for a month, I left her in a huff.

Fash. Well, well, I'll answer for it she'll soon resume her power, especially as friendship will prevent your pursuing the other too far. —But my coxcomb of a brother is an admirer of Amanda's too, is he?

Col. Town. Yes, and I believe is most heartily despised by her. But come with me, and you shall see her and your old friend Loveless.

Fash. I must pay my respects to his lordship—perhaps you can direct me to his lodgings.

Col. Town. Come with me; I shall pass by it.

Fash. I wish you could pay this visit for me, or could tell me what I should say to him.

Col. Town. Say nothing to him—apply yourself to his bag, his sword, his feather, his snuff-box; and when you are well with them, desire him to lend you a thousand pounds, and I'll engage you prosper.

Fash. 'Sdeath and furies! why was that coxcomb thrust intothe world before me? O Fortune, Fortune, thou art a jilt, by Gad!

[*Exeunt.*

SCENE II. —LORD FOPPINGTON'S *Dressing-room.*

Enter LORD FOPPINGTON *in his dressing-gown, and* LA VAROLE.

Lord Fop. [*Aside.*] Well, 'tis an unspeakable pleasure to be a man of quality—strike me dumb! Even the boors of this northern spa have learned the respect due to a title. —

[*Aloud.*] La Varole!

La Var. Milor—

Lord Fop. You ha'n't yet been at Muddymoat Hall, to announce my arrival, have you?

La Var. Not yet, milor.

Lord Fop. Then you need not go till Saturday-[*Exit* LA VAROLE] as I am in no particular haste to view my intended sposa. I shall sacrifice a day or two more to the pursuit of my friend Loveless's wife.

Amanda is a charming creature—strike me ugly! and, if I have any discernment in the world, she thinks no less of my Lord Foppington.

Re-enter LA VAROLE.

La Var. Milor, de shoemaker, de tailor, de hosier, de sempstress, de peru, be all ready, if your lordship please to dress.

Lord Fop. 'Tis well, admit them.

La Var. Hey, messieurs, entrez!

Enter TAILOR, SHOEMAKER, SEMPSTRESS, JEWELLER, *and* MENDLEGS.

Lord Fop. So, gentlemen, I hope you have all taken pains to show yourselves masters in your professions?

Tai. I think I may presume, sir—

La Var. Milor, you clown, you!

Tai. My lord—I ask your lordship's—pardon, my lord. I hope, my lord, your lordship will be pleased to own I have brought your lordship as accomplished a suit of clothes as ever peer of England wore, my lord—will your lordship please to view 'em now?

Lord Fop. Ay; but let my people dispose the glasses so that I may see myself before and behind; for I love to see myself all round. [*Puts on his clothes.*]

Enter TOM FASHION *and* LORY. *They remain behind, conversing apart.*

Fash. Heyday! what the devil have we here? Sure my gentleman's grown a favourite at court, he has got so many people at his levee.

Lory. Sir, these people come in order to make him a favourite at court—they are to establish him with the ladies.

Fash. Good Heaven! to what an ebb of taste are women fallen, that it should be in the power of a laced coat to recommend a gallant to them?

Lory. Sir, tailors and hair-dressers debauch all the women.

Fash. Thou sayest true. But now for my reception.

Lord Fop. [*To* TAILOR.] Death and eternal tortures!

Sir—I say the coat is too wide here by a foot.

Tai. My lord, if it had been tighter, 'twould neither have hooked nor buttoned.

Lord Fop. Rat the hooks and buttons, sir! Can any thing be worse than this? As Gad shall jedge me, it hangs on my shoulders like a chairman's surtout.

Tai. 'Tis not for me to dispute your lordship's fancy.

Lory. There, sir, observe what respect does.

Fash. Respect! damn him for a coxcomb! —But let's accost him. — [*Coming forward.*] Brother, I'm your humble servant.

Lord Fop. O Lard, Tam! I did not expect you in England. —Brother, I'm glad to see you. —But what has brought you to Scarborough, Tam! —[*To the* TAILOR.] Look you, sir, I shall never be reconciled to this nauseous wrapping-gown, therefore pray get me another suit with all possible expedition; for this is my eternal aversion. —[*Exit* TAILOR.] Well but, Tam, you don't tell me what has driven you to Scarborough. — Mrs. Calico, are not you of my mind?

Semp. Directly, my lord. —I hope your lordship is pleased with your ruffles?

Lord Fop. In love with them, stap my vitals! —Bring my bill, you shall be paid to-morrow.

Semp. I humbly thank your worship. [Exit.]

Lord Fop. Hark thee, shoemaker, these shoes aren't ugly, but they don't fit me.

Shoe. My lord, I think they fit you very well.

Lord Fop. They hurt me just below the instep.

Shoe. [*Feels his foot.*] No, my lord, they don't hurt you there.

Lord Fop. I tell thee they pinch me execrably.

Shoe. Why then, my lord, if those shoes pinch you, I'll be damned.

Lord Fop. Why, will thou undertake to persuade me I cannot feel?

Shoe. Your lordship may please to feel what you think fit, but that shoe does not hurt you—I think I understand my trade.

Lord Fop. Now, by all that's good and powerful, thou art an incomprehensive coxcomb! —but thou makest good shoes, and so I'll bear with thee.

Shoe. My lord, I have worked for half the people of quality in this town these twenty years, and 'tis very hard I shouldn't know when a shoe hurts, and when it don't.

Lord Fop. Well, pr'ythee be gone about thy business. —

[*Exit* SHOEMAKER.] Mr. Mendlegs, a word with you. —The calves of these stockings are thickened a little too much; they make my legs look like a porter's.

Mend. My lord, methinks they look mighty well.

Lord Fop. Ay, but you are not so good a judge of those things as I am—I have studied them all my life—therefore pray let the next be the thickness of a crown-piece less.

Mend. Indeed, my lord, they are the same kind I had the honour to furnish your lordship with in town.

Lord Fop. Very possibly, Mr. Mendlegs; but that was in the beginning of the winter, and you should always remember, Mr. Hosier, that if you make a nobleman's spring legs as robust as his autumnal calves, you commit a monstrous impropriety, and make no allowance Tor the fatigues of the winter. [*Exit*— MENDLEGS.]

Jewel. I hope, my lord, these buckles have had the unspeakable satisfaction of being honoured with your lordship's approbation?

Lord Fop. Why, they are of a pretty fancy; but don't you think them rather of the smallest?

Jewel. My lord, they could not well be larger, to keep on your lordship's shoe.

Lord Fop. My good sir, you forget that these matters are not as they used to be; formerly, indeed, the buckle was a sort of machine, intended to keep on the shoe; but the case is now quite reversed, and the shoe is of no earthly use, but to keep on the buckle. —Now give me my watches [SERVANT *fetches the watches,*] my chapeau, [SERVANT *brings a dress hat,*] my handkerchief, [SERVANT *pours some scented liquor on a handkerchief and brings it,*] my snuff-box [SERVANT *brings snuff-box.*] There, now the business of the morning is pretty well over. [*Exit* JEWELLER.]

Fash. [*Aside to* LORY.] Well, Lory, what dost think on't? —a very friendly reception from a brother, after three years' absence!

Lory. [*Aside to* TOM FASHION.] Why, sir, 'tis your own fault—here you have stood ever since you came in, and have not commended any one thing that belongs to him. [SERVANTS *all go off.*]

Fash. [*Aside to* LORY.] Nor ever shall, while they belong to a coxcomb. —[*To* LORD FOPPINGTON.] Now your people of business are gone, brother, I hope I may obtain a quarter of an hour's audience of you?

Lord Fop. Faith, Tam, I must beg you'll excuse me at this time, for I have an engagement which I would not break for the salvation of mankind. —Hey! —there! —is my carriage at the door? —You'll excuse me, brother. [*Going.*]

10

Fash. Shall you be back to dinner?

Lord Fop. As Gad shall jedge me, I can't tell; for it is passible I may dine with some friends at Donner's.

Fash. Shall I meet you there? For I must needs talk with you.

Lord Fop. That I'm afraid mayn't be quite so praper; for those I commonly eat with are people of nice conversation; and you know, Tam, your education has been a little at large. —But there are other ordinaries in town—very good beef ordinaries—I suppose, Tam, you can eat beef? —However, dear Tam, I'm glad to see thee in England, stap my vitals!

[*Exit,* LA VAROLE *following.*]

Fash. Hell and furies! is this to be borne?

Lory. Faith, sir, I could almost have given him a knock o' the pate myself.

Fash. 'Tis enough; I will now show you the excess of my passion, by being very calm. —Come, Lory, lay your loggerhead to mine, and, in cold blood, let us contrive his destruction.

Lory. Here comes a head, sir, would contrive it better than both our loggerheads, if she would but join in the confederacy.

Fash. By this light, Madam Coupler! she seems dissatisfied at something: let us observe her.

Enter MRS. COUPLER.

Mrs. Coup. So! I am likely to be well rewarded for my services, truly; my suspicions, I find, were but too just. — What! refuse to advance me a petty sum, when I am upon the point of making him master of a galleon! but let him look to the consequences; an ungrateful, narrow-minded coxcomb.

Fash. So he is, upon my soul, old lady; it must be my brother you speak of. *Mrs. Coup.* Ha! stripling, how came you here? What, hast spent all, eh? And art thou come to dun his lordship for assistance?

Fash. No, I want somebody's assistance to cut his lordship's throat, without the risk of being hanged for him.

Mrs. Coup. Egad, sirrah, I could help thee to do him almost as good a turn, without the danger of being burned in the hand for't.

Fash. How—how, old Mischief?

Mrs. Coup. Why, you must know I have done you the kindness to make up a match for your brother.

Fash. I am very much beholden to you, truly!

Mrs. Coup. You may be before the wedding-day, yet: the lady is a great heiress, the match is concluded, the writings are drawn, and his lordship is come hither to put the finishing hand to the business.

Fash. I understand as much.

Mrs. Coup. Now, you must know, stripling, your brother's a knave.

Fash. Good.

Mrs. Coup. He has given me a bond of a thousand pounds for helping him to this fortune, and has promised me as much more, in ready money, upon the day of the marriage; which, I understand by a friend, he never designs to pay me; and his just now refusing to pay me a part is a proof of it. If, therefore, you will be a generous young rogue, and secure me five thousand pounds, I'll help you to the lady.

Fash. And how the devil wilt thou do that?

Mrs. Coup. Without the devil's aid, I warrant thee. Thy brother's face not one of the family ever saw; the whole business has been managed by me, and all his letters go through my hands. Sir Tunbelly Clumsy, my relation—for that's the old gentleman's name—is apprised of his lordship's being down here, and expects him to-morrow to receive his daughter's hand; but the peer, I find, means to bait here a few days longer, to recover the fatigue of his journey, I suppose. Now you shall go to Muddymoat Hall in his place. —I'll give you a letter of introduction: and if you don't marry the girl before sunset, you deserve to be hanged before morning.

Fash. Agreed! agreed! and for thy reward—

Mrs. Coup. Well, well; —though I warrant thou hast not a farthing of money in thy pocket now—no—one may see it in thy face.

Fash. Not a sous, by Jupiter!

Mrs. Coup. Must I advance, then? Well, be at my lodgings, next door, this evening, and I'll see what may be done—we'll sign and seal, and when I have given thee some further instructions, thou shalt hoist sail and be one.

[*Exit.*]

Fash. So, Lory, Fortune, thou seest, at last takes care of merit! we are in a fair way to be great people.

Lory. Ay, sir, if the devil don't step between the cup and the lip, as he used to do.

Fash. Why, faith, he has played me many a damned trick to spoil my fortune; and, egad, I am almost afraid he's at work about it again now; but if I should tell thee how, thou'dst wonder at me.

Lory. Indeed, sir, I should not.

Fash. How dost know?

Lory. Because, sir, I have wondered at you so often, I can wonder at you no more.

Fash. No! what wouldst thou say, if a qualm of conscience should spoil my design?

Lory. I would eat my words, and wonder more than ever.

Fash. Why faith, Lory, though I have played many a roguish trick, this is so full-grown a cheat, I find I must take pains to come up to't—I have scruples.

Lory. They are strong symptoms of death. If you find they increase, sir, pray make your will.

Fash. No, my conscience shan't starve me neither: but thus far I'll listen to it. Before I execute this project, I'll try my brother to the bottom. If he has yet so much humanity about him as to assist me—though with a moderate aid—I'll drop my project at his feet, and show him how I can do for him much more than what I'd ask he'd do for me. This one conclusive trial of him I resolve to make. Succeed or fail, still victory is my lot; If I subdue his heart, 'tis well—if not, I will subdue my conscience to my plot.

[*Exeunt.*]

ACT II.

SCENE I. —LOVELESS'S *Lodgings*.

Enter LOVELESS *and* AMANDA.

Love. How do you like these lodgings, my dear? For my part, I am so pleased with them, I shall hardly remove whilst we stay here, if you are satisfied.

Aman. I am satisfied with everything that pleases you, else I had not come to Scarborough at all.

Love. Oh, a little of the noise and folly of this place will sweeten the pleasures of our retreat; we shall find the charms of our retirement doubled when we return to it.

Aman. That pleasing prospect will be my chiefest entertainment, whilst, much against my will, I engage in those empty pleasures which 'tis so much the fashion to be fond of.

Love. I own most of them are, indeed, but empty; yet there are delights of which a private life is destitute, which may divert an honest man, and be a harmless entertainment to a virtuous woman: good music is one; and truly (with some small allowance) the plays, I think, may be esteemed another.

Aman. Plays, I must confess, have some small charms. What do you think of that you saw last night?

Love. To say truth, I did not mind it much—my attention was for some time taken off to admire the workmanship of Nature in the face of a young lady who sat at some distance from me, she was so exquisitely handsome.

Aman. So exquisitely handsome!

Love. Why do you repeat my words, my dear?

15

Aman. Because you seemed to speak them with such pleasure, I thought I might oblige you with their echo.

Love. Then you are alarmed, Amanda?

Aman. It is my duty to be so when you are in danger.

Love. You are too quick in apprehending for me. I viewed her with a world of admiration, but not one glance of love.

Aman. Take heed of trusting to such nice distinctions. But were your eyes the only things that were inquisitive? Had I been in your place, my tongue, I fancy, had been curious too. I should have asked her where she lived—yet still without design—who was she, pray?

Love. Indeed I cannot tell.

Aman. You will not tell.

Love. Upon my honour, then, I did not ask.

Aman. Nor do you know what company was with her?

Love. I do not. But why are you so earnest?

Aman. I thought I had cause.

Love. But you thought wrong, Amanda; for turn the case, and let it be your story: should you come home and tell me you had seen a handsome man, should I grow jealous because you had eyes?

Aman. But should I tell you he was exquisitely so, and that I had gazed on him with admiration, should you not think 'twere possible I might go one step further, and inquire his name?

Love. [*Aside.*] She has reason on her side; I have talked too much; but I must turn off another way. — [*Aloud.*] Will you then make no difference, Amanda, between the language of our sex and yours? There is a modesty restrains your tongues, which makes you speak by halves when you commend; but roving flattery gives a loose to ours, which makes us still speak double what we think.

Enter SERVANT.

Ser. Madam, there is a lady at the door in a chair desires to know whether your ladyship sees company; her name is Berinthia.

Aman. Oh dear! 'tis a relation I have not seen these five years; pray her to walk in. —[*Exit* SERVANT.] Here's another beauty for you; she was, when I saw her last, reckoned extremely handsome.

Love. Don't be jealous now; for I shall gaze upon her too.

Enter BERINTHIA.

Ha! by heavens, the very woman! [*Aside.*]

Ber. [*Salutes* AMANDA.] Dear Amanda, I did not expect to meet you in Scarborough.

Aman. Sweet cousin, I'm overjoyed to see you. —Mr. Loveless, here's a relation and a friend of mine, I desire you'll be better acquainted with.

Love. [*Salutes* BERINTHIA.] If my wife never desires a harder thing, madam, her request will be easily granted.

Re-enter SERVANT.

Ser. Sir, my Lord Foppington presents his humble service to you, and desires to know how you do. He's at the next door; and, if it be not inconvenient to you, he'll come and wait upon you.

Love. Give my compliments to his lordship, and I shall be glad to see him. —[*Exit* SERVANT.] If you are not acquainted with his lordship, madam, you will be entertained with his character.

Aman. Now it moves my pity more than my mirth to see a man whom nature has made no fool be so very industrious to pass for an ass.

Love. No, there you are wrong, Amanda; you should never bestow your pity upon those who take pains for your contempt: pity those whom nature abuses, never those who abuse nature.

Enter LORD FOPPINGTON.

Lord Fop. Dear Loveless, I am your most humble servant.

Love. My lord, I'm yours.

Lord Fop. Madam, your ladyship's very obedient slave.

Love. My lord, this lady is a relation of my wife's.

Lord Fop. [*Salutes* BERINTHIA.] The beautifullest race of people upon earth, rat me! Dear Loveless, I am overjoyed that you think of continuing here: I am, stap my vitals! — [*To* AMANDA.] For Gad's sake, madam, how has your ladyship been able to subsist thus long, under the fatigue of a country life?

Aman. My life has been very far from that, my lord; it has been a very quiet one.

Lord Fop. Why, that's the fatigue I speak of, madam; for 'tis impossible to be quiet without thinking: now thinking is to me the greatest fatigue in the world.

Aman. Does not your lordship love reading, then?

Lord Fop. Oh, passionately, madam; but I never think of what I read. For example, madam, my life is a perpetual stream of pleasure, that glides through with such a variety of entertainments, I believe the wisest of our ancestors never had the least conception of any of 'em. I rise, madam, when in town, about twelve o'clock. I don't rise sooner, because it is the worst thing in the world for the complexion: not that I pretend to be a beau; but a man must endeavour to look decent, lest he makes so odious a figure in the side-bax, the ladies should be compelled to turn their eyes upon the play. So at twelve o'clock, I say, I rise. Naw, if I find it is a good day, I resalve to take the exercise of riding; so drink my chocolate, and draw on my boots by two. On my return, I dress; and, after dinner, lounge perhaps to the opera.

Ber. Your lordship, I suppose, is fond of music?

Lord Fop. Oh, passionately, on Tuesdays and Saturdays; for then there is always the best company, and one is not expected to undergo the fatigue of listening.

Aman. Does your lordship think that the case at the opera?

Lord Fop. Most certainly, madam. There is my Lady Tattle, my Lady Prate, my Lady Titter, my Lady Sneer, my Lady Giggle, and my Lady Grin—these have boxes in the front, and while any favourite air is singing, are the prettiest company in the waurld, stap my vitals! —Mayn't we hope for the honour to see you added to our society, madam?

Aman. Alas! my lord, I am the worst company in the world at a concert, I'm so apt to attend to the music.

Lord Fop. Why, madam, that is very pardonable in the country or at church, but a monstrous inattention in a polite assembly. But I am afraid I tire the company?

Love. Not at all. Pray go on.

Lord Fop. Why then, ladies, there only remains to add, that I generally conclude the evening at one or other of the clubs; nat that I ever play deep; indeed I have been for some time tied up from losing above five thousand paunds at a sitting.

Love. But isn't your lordship sometimes obliged to attend the weighty affairs of the nation?

Lord Fop. Sir, as to weighty affairs, I leave them to weighty heads; I never intend mine shall be a burden to my body.

Ber. Nay, my lord, but you are a pillar of the state.

Lord Fop. An ornamental pillar, madam; for sooner than undergo any part of the fatigue, rat me, but the whole building should fall plump to the ground!

Aman. But, my lord, a fine gentleman spends a great deal of his time in his intrigues; you have given us no account of them yet.

Lord Fop. [*Aside.*] So! she would inquire into my amours—that's jealousy, poor soul! —I see she's in love with me. —[*Aloud.*] O Lord, madam, I had like to have forgot a secret I must need tell your ladyship. —Ned, you must not be so jealous now as to listen.

Love. [*Leading* BERINTHIA *up the stage.*] Not I, my lord; I am too fashionable a husband to pry into the secrets of my wife.

Lord Fop. [*Aside to* AMANDA *squeezing her hand.*] I am in love with you to desperation, strike me speechless!

Aman. [*Strikes him on the ear.*] Then thus I return your passion. —An impudent fool!

Lord Fop. God's curse, madam, I am a peer of the realm!

Love. [*Hastily returning.*] Hey! what the devil, do you affront my wife, sir? Nay, then— [*Draws. They fight.*]

Aman. What has my folly done? —Help! murder! help! Part them for Heaven's sake.

Lord Fop. [*Falls back and leans on his sword.*] Ah! quite through the body, stap my vitals!

Enter SERVANTS.

Love. [*Runs to* LORD FOPPINGTON.] I hope I ha'nt killed the fool, however. Bear him up. —Call a surgeon there.

Lord Fop. Ay, pray make haste. [*Exit* SERVANT.

Love. This mischief you may thank yourself for.

Lord Fop. I may say so; love's the devil indeed, Ned.

Re-enter SERVANT, *with* PROBE.

Ser. Here's Mr. Probe, sir, was just going by the door.

Lord Fop. He's the welcomest man alive.

Probe. Stand by, stand by, stand by; pray, gentlemen, stand by. Lord have mercy upon us, did you never see a man run through the body before? —Pray stand by.

Lord Fop. Ah, Mr. Probe, I'm a dead man.

Probe. A dead man, and I by! I should laugh to see that, egad.

Love. Pr'ythee don't stand prating, but look upon his wound.

Probe. Why, what if I don't look upon his wound this hour, sir?

Love. Why, then he'll bleed to death, sir.

Probe. Why, then I'll fetch him to life again, sir.

Love. 'Slife! he's run through the body, I tell thee.

Probe. I wish he was run through the heart, and I should get the more credit by his cure. Now I hope you are satisfied? Come, now let me come at him—now let me come at him. — [*Viewing his wound.*] Oops I what a gash is here! why, sir, a man may drive a coach and six horses into your body.

Lord Fop. Oh!

Probe. Why, what the devil have you run the gentleman through with—a scythe? —[*Aside.*] A little scratch between the skin and the ribs, that's all.

Love. Let me see his wound.

Probe. Then you shall dress it, sir; for if anybody looks upon it I won't.

Love. Why, thou art the veriest coxcomb I ever saw!

Probe. Sir, I am not master of my trade for nothing.

Lord Fop. Surgeon!

Probe. Sir.

Lord Fop. Are there any hopes?

Probe. Hopes! I can't tell. What are you willing to give for a cure?
Lord Fop. Five hundred paunds with pleasure.

Probe. Why then perhaps there may be hopes; but we must avoid further delay. —Here, help the gentleman into a chair, and carry him to my house presently—that's the properest place— [*Aside.*] to bubble him out of his money. —[*Aloud.*] Come, a chair—a chair quickly—there, in with him. [SERVANTS *put* LORD FOPPINGTON *into a chair.*]

Lord Fop. Dear Loveless, adieu; if I die, I forgive thee; and if I live, I hope thou wilt do as much by me. I am sorry you and I should quarrel, but I hope here's an end on't; for if you are satisfied, I am.

Love. I shall hardly think it worth my prosecuting any further, so you may be at rest, sir.

Lord Fop. Thou art a generous fellow, strike me dumb! —[*Aside.*] But thou hast an impertinent wife, stap my vitals!

Probe. So—carry him off! —carry him off! —We shall have him into a fever by-and-by. —Carry him off! [*Exit with* LORD FOPPINGTON.]

Enter COLONEL TOWNLY.

Col. Town. So, so, I am glad to find you all alive. —I met a wounded peer carrying off. For heaven's sake what was the matter?

Love. Oh, a trifle! he would have made love to my wife before my face, so she obliged him with a box o' the ear, and I ran him through the body, that was all.

Col. Town. Bagatelle on all sides. But pray, madam, how long has this noble lord been an humble servant of yours?

Aman. This is the first I have heard on't—so I suppose, 'tis his quality more than his love has brought him into this adventure. He thinks his title an authentic passport to every woman's heart below the degree of a peeress.

Col. Town. He's coxcomb enough to think anything: but I would not have you brought into trouble for him. I hope there's no danger of his life?

Love. None at all. He's fallen into the hands of a roguish surgeon, who, I perceive, designs to frighten a little money out of him: but I saw his wound—'tis nothing: he may go to the ball to-night if he pleases.

Col. Town. I am glad you have corrected him without further mischief, or you might have deprived me of the pleasure of executing a plot against his lordship, which I have been contriving with an old acquaintance of yours.

Love. Explain.

Col. Town. His brother, Tom Fashion, is come down here, and we have it in contemplation to save him the trouble of his intended wedding: but we want your assistance. Tom would have called but he is preparing for his enterprise, so I promised to bring you to him—so, sir, if these ladies can spare you—

Love. I'll go with you with all my heart. —[*Aside.*] Though I could wish, methinks, to stay and gaze a little longer on that creature. Good gods! how engaging she is! —but what have I to do with beauty? I have already had my portion, and must not covet more.

Aman. Mr. Loveless, pray one word with you before you go.

[*Exit* COLONEL TOWNLY.

Love. What would my dear?

Aman. Only a woman's foolish question: how do you like my cousin here?

Love. Jealous already, Amanda?

Aman. Not at all: I ask you for another reason.

Love. [*Aside.*] Whate'er her reason be, I must not tell her true. — [*Aloud.*] Why, I confess, she's handsome: but you must not think I slight your kinswoman, if I own to you, of all the women who may claim that character, she is the last that would triumph in my heart.

Aman. I'm satisfied.

Love. Now tell me why you asked?

Aman. At night I will—adieu!

Love. I'm yours. [*Kisses her and exit.*]

Aman. I'm glad to find he does not like her, for I have a great mind to persuade her to come and live with me. [*Aside.*]

Ber. So! I find my colonel continues in his airs; there must be something more at the bottom of this than the provocation he pretends from me. [*Aside.*]

Aman. For Heaven's sake, Berinthia, tell me what way I shall take to persuade you to come and live with me.

Ber. Why, one way in the world there is, and but one.

Aman. And pray what is that?

Ber. It is to assure me—I shall be very welcome.

Aman. If that be all, you shall e'en sleep here to-night.

Ber. To-night.

Aman. Yes, to-night.

Ber. Why, the people where I lodge will think me mad.

Aman. Let 'em think what they please.

Ber. Say you so, Amanda? Why, then, they shall think what they please: for I'm a young widow, and I care not what anybody thinks. —Ah, Amanda, it's a delicious thing to be a young widow!

Aman. You'll hardly make me think so.

Ber. Poh! because you are in love with your husband.

Aman. Pray, 'tis with a world of innocence I would inquire whether you think those we call women of reputation do really escape all other men as they do those shadows of beaux.

Ber. Oh no, Amanda; there are a sort of men make dreadful work amongst 'em, men that may be called the beau's antipathy, for they agree in nothing but walking upon two legs. These have brains, the beau has none. These are in love with their mistress, the beau with himself. They take care of their reputation, the beau is industrious to destroy it. They are decent, he's a fop; in short, they are men, he's an ass.

Aman. If this be their character, I fancy we had here, e'en now, a pattern of 'em both.

Ber. His lordship and Colonel Townly?

Aman. The same.

Ber. As for the lord, he is eminently so; and for the other, I can assure you there's not a man in town who has a better interest with the women that are worth having an interest with.

Aman. He answers the opinion I had ever of him. [*Takes her hand.*] I must acquaint you with a secret—'tis not that fool alone has talked to me of love; Townly has been tampering too.

Ber. [*Aside.*] So, so! here the mystery comes out! — [*Aloud.*] Colonel Townly! impossible, my dear!

25

Aman. 'Tis true indeed; though he has done it in vain; nor do I think that all the merit of mankind combined could shake the tender love I bear my husband; yet I will own to you, Berinthia, I did not start at his addresses, as when they came from one whom I contemned.

Ber. [*Aside.*] Oh, this is better and better! — [*Aloud.*] Well said, Innocence! and you really think, my dear, that nothing could abate your constancy and attachment to your husband?

Aman. Nothing, I am convinced.

Ber. What, if you found he loved another woman better?

Aman. Well!

Ber. Well! —why, were I that thing they call a slighted wife, somebody should run the risk of being that thing they call—a husband. Don't I talk madly?

Aman. Madly indeed!

Ber. Yet I'm very innocent.

Aman. That I dare swear you are. I know how to make allowances for your humour: but you resolve then never to marry again?

Ber. Oh no! I resolve I will.

Aman. How so?

Ber. That I never may.

Aman. You banter me.

Ber. Indeed I don't: but I consider I'm a woman, and form my resolutions accordingly.

Aman. Well, my opinion is, form what resolutions you will, matrimony will be the end on't.

Ber. I doubt it—but a—Heavens! I have business at home, and am half an hour too late.

Aman. As you are to return with me, I'll just give some orders, and walk with you.

Ber. Well, make haste, and we'll finish this subject as we go—[*Exit* AMANDA.]. Ah, poor Amanda! you have led a country life. Well, this discovery is lucky! Base Townly! at once false to me and treacherous to his friend! —And my innocent and demure cousin too! I have it in my power to be revenged on her, however. Her husband, if I have any skill in countenance, would be as happy in my smiles as Townly can hope to be in hers. I'll make the experiment, come what will on't. The woman who can forgive the being robbed of a favoured lover, must be either an idiot or a wanton. [*Exit.*]

ACT III.

SCENE I. —LORD FOPPINGTON's *Lodgings.*

Enter LORD FOPPINGTON, *and* LA VAROLE.

Lord Fop. Hey, fellow, let thy vis-a-vis come to the door.

La Var. Will your lordship venture so soon to expose yourself to the weather?

Lord Fop. Sir, I will venture as soon as I can expose myself to the ladies.

La Var. I wish your lordship would please to keep house a little longer; I'm afraid your honour does not well consider your wound.

Lord Fop. My wound! —I would not be in eclipse another day, though I had as many wounds in my body as I have had in my heart. So mind, Varole, let these cards be left as directed; for this evening I shall wait on my future father-in-law, Sir Tunbelly, and I mean to commence my devoirs to the lady, by giving an entertainment at her father's expense; and hark thee, tell Mr. Loveless I request he and his company will honour me with their presence, or I shall think we are not friends.

La Var. I will be sure, milor. [*Exit.*]

Enter TOM FASHION.

Fash. Brother, your servant; how do you find yourself to-day?

Lord Fop. So well that I have ardered my coach to the door—so there's no danger of death this baut, Tam.

Fash. I'm very glad of it.

Lord Fop. [*Aside.*] That I believe a lie. — [*Aloud.*] Pr'ythee, Tam, tell me one thing—did not your heart cut a caper up to your mauth, when you heard I was run through the bady?

Fash. Why do you think it should?

Lord Fop. Because I remember mine did so when I heard my uncle was shot through the head.

Fash. It, then, did very ill.

Lord Fop. Pr'ythee, why so?

Fash. Because he used you very well.

Lord Fop. Well! —Naw, strike me dumb! he starved me; he has let me want a thausand women for want of a thausand paund.

Fash. Then he hindered you from making a great many ill bargains; for I think no woman worth money that will take money.

Lord Fop. If I was a younger brother I should think so too.

Fash. Then you are seldom much in love?

Lord Fop. Never, stap my vitals!

Fash. Why, then, did you make all this bustle about Amanda?

Lord Fop. Because she's a woman of insolent virtue, and I thought myself piqued in honour to debauch her.

Fash. Very well. —[*Aside.*] Here's a rare fellow for you, to have the spending of ten thousand pounds a year! But now for my business with him. —[*Aloud.*] Brother, though I know to talk of any business (especially of money) is a theme not quite so entertaining to you as that of the ladies, my necessities are such, I hope you'll have patience to hear me.

Lord Fop. The greatness of your necessities, Tam, is the worst argument in the waurld for your being patiently heard. I do believe you are going to make a very good speech, but, strike me dumb! it has the worst beginning of any speech I have heard this twelvemonth.

Fash. I'm sorry you think so.

Lord Fop. I do believe thou art: but, come, let's know the affair quickly.

Fash. Why, then, my case, in a word, is this: the necessary expenses of my travels have so much exceeded the wretched income of my annuity, that I have been forced to mortgage it for five hundred pounds, which is spent. So unless you are so kind as to assist me in redeeming it, I know no remedy but to take a purse.

Lord Fop. Why, faith, Tam, to give you my sense of the thing, I do think taking a purse the best remedy in the waurld; for if you succeed, you are relieved that way, if you are taken [*Drawing his hand round his neck*], you are relieved t'other.

Fash. I'm glad to see you are in so pleasant a humour; I hope I shall find the effects on't.

Lord Fop. Why, do you then really think it a reasonable thing, that I should give you five hundred paunds?

Fash. I do not ask it as a due, brother; I am willing to receive it as a favour.

Lord Fop. Then thou art willing to receive it anyhow, strike me speechless! But these are damned times to give money in; taxes are so great, repairs so exorbitant, tenants such rogues, and bouquets so dear, that the devil take me I'm reduced to that extremity in my cash, I have been forced to retrench in that one article of sweet pawder, till I have brought it down to five guineas a maunth—now judge, Tam, whether I can spare you five paunds.

Fash. If you can't I must starve, that's all. — [*Aside.*] Damn him!

Lord Fop. All I can say is, you should have been a better husband.

Fash. Ouns! if you can't live upon ten thousand a year, how do you think I should do't upon two hundred?

Lord Fop. Don't be in a passion, Tam, for passion is the most unbecoming thing in the waurld—to the face. Look you, I don't love to say anything to you to make you melancholy, but upon this occasion I must take leave to put you in mind that a running horse does require more attendance than a coach-horse. Nature has made some difference twixt you and me.

Fash. Yes—she has made you older. —[*Aside.*] Plague take her.

Lord Fop. That is not all, Tam.

Fash. Why, what is there else?

Lord Fop. [*Looks first on himself and then on his brother.*] Ask the ladies.

Fash. Why, thou essence-bottle, thou musk-cat! dost thou then think thou hast any advantage over me but what Fortune has given thee?

Lord Fop. I do, stap my vitals!

Fash. Now, by all that's great and powerful, thou art the prince of coxcombs!

Lord Fop. Sir, I am proud at being at the head of so prevailing a party.

Fash. Will nothing provoke thee? —Draw, coward!

Lord Fop. Look you, Tam, you know I have always taken you for a mighty dull fellow, and here is one of the foolishest plats broke out that I have seen a lang time. Your poverty makes life so burdensome to you, you would provoke me to a quarrel, in hopes either to slip through my lungs into my estate, or to get yourself run through the guts, to put an end to your pain. But I will disappoint you in both your designs; far, with the temper of a philasapher, and the discretion of a statesman—I shall leave the room with my sword in the scabbard. [*Exit.*]

Fash. So! farewell, brother; and now, conscience, I defy thee. Lory!

Enter LORY.

Lory. Sir!

Fash. Here's rare news, Lory; his lordship has given me a pill has purged off all my scruples.

Lory. Then my heart's at ease again: for I have been in a lamentable fright, sir, ever since your conscience had the impudence to intrude into your company.

Fash. Be at peace; it will come there no more: my brother has given it a wring by the nose, and I have kicked it downstairs. So run away to the inn, get the chaise ready quickly, and bring it to Dame Coupler's without a moment's delay.

Lory. Then, sir, you are going straight about the fortune?

Fash. I am. —Away—fly, Lory!

Lory. The happiest day I ever saw. I'm upon the wing already. Now then I shall get my wages. [*Exeunt.*]

SCENE II. —*A Garden behind* LOVELESS'S *Lodgings.*

Enter LOVELESS *and* SERVANT.

Love. Is my wife within?

Ser. No, sir, she has gone out this half-hour.

Love. Well, leave me. —[*Exit* SERVANT.] How strangely does my mind run on this widow! —Never was my heart so suddenly seized on before. That my wife should pick out her, of all womankind, to be her playfellow! But what fate does, let fate answer for: I sought it not. So! by Heavens! here she comes.

Enter BERINTHIA.

Ber. What makes you look so thoughtful, sir? I hope you are not ill.

Love. I was debating, madam, whether I was so or not, and that was it which made me look so thoughtful.

Ber. Is it then so hard a matter to decide? I thought all people were acquainted with their own bodies, though few people know their own minds.

Love. What if the distemper I suspect be in the mind?

Ber. Why then I'll undertake to prescribe you a cure.

Love. Alas! you undertake you know not what.

Ber. So far at least, then, you allow me to be a physician.

Love. Nay, I'll allow you to be so yet further: for I have reason to believe, should I put myself into your hands, you would increase my distemper.

Ber. How?

Love. Oh, you might betray me to my wife.

Ber. And so lose all my practice.

Love. Will you then keep my secret?

Ber. I will.

Love. Well—but swear it.

Ber. I swear by woman.

Love. Nay, that's swearing by my deity; swear by your own, and I shall believe you.

Ber. Well then, I swear by man!

Love. I'm satisfied. Now hear my symptoms, and give me your advice. The first were these; when I saw you at the play, a random glance you threw at first alarmed me. I could not turn my eyes from whence the danger came—I gazed upon you till my heart began to pant—nay, even now, on your approaching me, my illness is so increased that if you do not help me I shall, whilst you look on, consume to ashes. [*Takes her hand.*]

Ber. O Lord, let me go! 'tis the plague, and we shall be infected. [Breaking from him.]

Love. Then we'll die together, my charming angel.

Ber. O Gad! the devil's in you! Lord, let me go! —here's somebody coming.

Re-enter SERVANT.

Ser. Sir, my lady's come home, and desires to speak with you.

Love. Tell her I'm coming. —[*Exit* SERVANT.] But before I go, one glass of nectar to drink her health. [*To* BERINTHIA.]

Ber. Stand off, or I shall hate you, by Heavens!

Love. [*Kissing her.*] In matters of love, a woman's oath is no more to be minded than a man's. [*Exit.*]

Ber. Um!

Enter COLONEL TOWNLY.

Col. Town. [*Aside.*] So? what's here—Berinthia and Loveless—and in such close conversation! —I cannot now wonder at her indifference in excusing herself to me! —O rare woman! —Well then, let Loveless look to his wife, 'twill be but the retort courteous on both sides. — [*Aloud.*] Your servant, madam; I need not ask you how you do, you have got so good a colour.

Ber. No better than I used to have, I suppose.

Col. Town. A little more blood in your cheeks.

Ber. I have been walking!

34

Col. Town. Is that all? Pray was it Mr. Loveless went from here just now?

Ber. O yes—he has been walking with me.

Col. Town. He has!

Ber. Upon my word I think he is a very agreeable man; and there is certainly something particularly insinuating in his address.

Col. Town. [*Aside.*] So, so! she hasn't even the modesty to dissemble! [*Aloud.*] Pray, madam, may I, without impertinence, trouble you with a few serious questions?

Ber. As many as you please; but pray let them be as little serious as possible.

Col. Town. Is it not near two years since I have presumed to address you?

Ber. I don't know exactly—but it has been a tedious long time.

Col. Town. Have I not, during that period, had every reason to believe that my assiduities were far from being unacceptable?

Ber. Why, to do you justice, you have been extremely troublesome— and I confess I have been more civil to you than you deserved.

Col. Town. Did I not come to this place at your express desire, and for no purpose but the honour of meeting you? —and after waiting a month in disappointment, have you condescended to explain, or in the slightest way apologise for, your conduct?

Ber. O heavens! apologise for my conduct! —apologise to you! O you barbarian! But pray now, my good serious colonel, have you anything more to add?

Col. Town. Nothing, madam, but that after such behaviour I am less surprised at what I saw just now; it is not very wonderful that the woman who can trifle with the delicate addresses of an honourable lover should be found coquetting with the husband of her friend.

Ber. Very true: no more wonderful than it was for this honourable lover to divert himself in the absence of this coquette, with endeavouring to seduce his friend's wife! O colonel, colonel, don't talk of honour or your friend, for Heaven's sake!

Col. Town. [*Aside.*] 'Sdeath! how came she to suspect this! —[*Aloud.*] Really, madam, I don't understand you.

Ber. Nay, nay, you saw I did not pretend to misunderstand you. — But here comes the lady; perhaps you would be glad to be left with her for an explanation.

Col. Town. O madam, this recrimination is a poor resource; and to convince you how much you are mistaken, I beg leave to decline the happiness you propose me. —Madam, your servant.

Enter AMANDA. COLONEL TOWNLY *whispers* AMANDA, *and exit.*

Ber. [*Aside.*] He carries it off well, however; upon my word, very well! How tenderly they part! —[*Aloud*] So, cousin; I hope you have not been chiding your admirer for being with me? I assure you we have been talking of you.

Aman. Fy, Berinthia! —my admirer! will you never learn to talk in earnest of anything?

Ber. Why this shall be in earnest, if you please; for my part, I only tell you matter of fact. *Aman.* I'm sure there's so much jest and earnest in what you say to me on this subject, I scarce know how to take it. I have just parted with Mr. Loveless; perhaps it is fancy, but I think there is an alteration in his manner which alarms me.

Ber. And so you are jealous; is that all?

Aman. That all! is jealousy, then, nothing?

Ber. It should be nothing, if I were in your case.

Aman. Why, what would you do?

Ber. I'd cure myself.

Aman. How?

Ber. Care as little for my husband as he did for me. Look you, Amanda, you may build castles in the air, and fume, and fret, and grow thin, and lean, and pale, and ugly, if you please; but I tell you, no man worth having is true to his wife, or ever was, or ever will be so.

Aman. Do you then really think he's false to me? for I did not suspect him.

Ber. Think so? I am sure of it.

Aman. You are sure on't?

Ber. Positively—he fell in love at the play.

Aman. Right—the very same. But who could have told you this?

Ber. Um! —Oh, Townly! I suppose your husband has made him his confidant.

Aman. O base Loveless! And what did Townly say on't?

Ber. [*Aside.*] So, so! why should she ask that? — [*Aloud.*] Say! why he abused Loveless extremely, and said all the tender things of you in the world.

Aman. Did he? —Oh! my heart! —I'm very ill—dear Berinthia, don't leave me a moment. [*Exeunt.*]

SCENE III. —*Outside of* SIR TUNRELLY CLUMSY'S *House.*

Enter TOM FASHION *and* LORY.

Fash. So here's our inheritance, Lory, if we can but get into possession. But methinks the seat of our family looks like Noah's ark, as if the chief part on't were designed for the fowls of the air, and the beasts of the field.

Lory. Pray, sir, don't let your head run upon the orders of building here: get but the heiress, let the devil take the house.

Fash. Get but the house, let the devil take the heiress! I say. —But come, we have no time to squander; knock at the door. —

[LORY *knocks two or three times at the gate.*] What the devil! have they got no ears in this house? —Knock harder.

Lory. Egad, sir, this will prove some enchanted castle; we shall have the giant come out by-and-by, with his club, and beat our brains out. [*Knocks again.*]

Fash. Hush, they come.

Ser. [Within.] Who is there?

Lory. Open the door and see: is that your country breeding?

Ser. Ay, but two words to that bargain. —Tummus, is the blunderbuss primed?

Fash. Ouns! give 'em good words, Lory, —or we shall be shot here a fortune catching.

Lory. Egad, sir, I think you're in the right on't. —Ho! Mr. What-d'ye-call-'um, will you please to let us in? or are we to be left to grow like willows by your moat side?

SERVANT *appears at the window with a blunderbuss.*

Ser. Well naw, what's ya're business?

Fash. Nothing, sir, but to wait upon Sir Tunbelly, with your leave.

Ser. To weat upon Sir Tunbelly! why, you'll find that's just as Sir Tunbelly pleases.

Fash. But will you do me the favour, sir, to know whether Sir Tunbelly pleases or not?

Ser. Why, look you, d'ye see, with good words much may be done. Ralph, go thy ways, and ask Sir Tunbelly if he pleases to be waited upon—and dost hear, call to nurse, that she may lock up Miss Hoyden before the gates open.

Fash. D'ye hear, that, Lory?

Enter SIR TUNBELLY CLUMSY, with SERVANTS, armed with guns, clubs, pitchforks, &c.

Lory. Oh! [*Runs behind his master.*] O Lord! O Lord! Lord! we are both dead men!

Fash. Fool! thy fear will, ruin us. [*Aside to LORY.*]

Lory. My fear, sir? 'sdeath, Sir, I fear nothing. — [*Aside.*] Would I were well up to the chin in a horse-pond!

Sir Tun. Who is it here hath any business with me?

Fash. Sir, 'tis I, if your name be Sir Tunbelly Clumsy.

Sir Tun. Sir, my name is Sir Tunbelly Clumsy, whether you have any business with me or not. —So you see I am not ashamed of my name, nor my face either.

Fash. Sir, you have no cause that I know of.

Sir Tun. Sir, if you have no cause either, I desire to know who you are; for, till I know your name, I shan't ask you to come into my house: and when I do know your name, 'tis six to four I don't ask you then.

Fash. Sir, I hope you'll find this letter an authentic passport. [*Gives him a letter.*]

Sir Tun. Cod's my life, from Mrs. Coupler! —I ask your lordship's pardon ten thousand times. —[*To a SERVANT.*] Here, run in a-doors quickly; get a Scotch coal fire in the parlour, set all the Turkey work chairs in their places, get the brass candlesticks out, and be sure stick the socket full of laurel—run! —[*Turns to TOM FASHION.*]—My lord, I ask your lordship's pardon. —[*To SERVANT.*] And, do you hear, run away to nurse; bid her let Miss Hoyden loose again. —[*Exit SERVANT.*] I hope your honour will excuse the disorder of my family. We are not used to receive men of your lordship's great quality every day. Pray, where are your coaches and servants, my lord?

Fash. Sir, that I might give you and your daughter a proof how impatient I am to be nearer akin to you, I left my equipage to follow me, and came away post with only one servant.

Sir Tun. Your lordship does me too much honour—it was exposing your person to too much fatigue and danger, I protest it was: but my daughter shall endeavour to make you what amends she can: and, though I say it that should not say it, Hoyden has charms.

Fash. Sir, I am not a stranger to them, though I am to her; common fame has done her justice.

Sir Tun. My lord, I am common fame's very grateful, humble servant. My lord, my girl's young—Hoyden is young, my lord: but this I must say for her, what she wants in art she has in breeding; and what's wanting in her age, is made good in her constitution. — So pray, my lord, walk in; pray, my lord, walk in. *Fash.* Sir, I wait upon you. [*Exeunt.*]

SCENE IV. —*A Room in* SIR TUNBELLY CLUMSY'S *House.*

MISS HOYDEN *discovered alone.*

Miss Hoyd. Sure, nobody was ever used as I am! I know well enough what other girls do, for all they think to make a fool o' me. It's well I have a husband a-coming, or ecod I'd marry the baker, I would so. Nobody can knock at the gate, but presently I must be locked up; and here's the young greyhound can run loose about the house all the day, so she can. —'Tis very well!

Nurse. [*Without opening the door.*] Miss Hoyden! miss, miss, miss! Miss Hoyden!

Enter NURSE.

Miss Hoyd. Well, what do you make such a noise for, eh? What do you din a body's ears for? Can't one be at quiet for you?

Nurse. What do I din your ears for? Here's one come wil din your ears for you.

Miss Hoyd. What care I who's come? I care not a fig who comes, or who goes, so long as I must be locked up like the ale-cellar.

Nurse. That, miss, is for fear you should be drank before you are ripe.

Miss Hoyd. Oh, don't trouble your head about that; I'm as ripe as you, though not so mellow.

Nurse. Very well! Now I have a good mind to lock you up again, and not let you see my lord to-night.

Miss Hoyd. My lord: why, is my husband come?

Nurse. Yes, marry, is he; and a goodly person too.

Miss Hoyd. [*Hugs* NURSE.] Oh, my dear nurse, forgive me this once, and I'll never misuse you again; no, if I do, you shall give me three thumps on the back, and a great pinch by the cheek.

Nurse. Ah, the poor thing! see now it melts; it's as full of good-nature as an egg's full of meat.

Miss Hoyd. But, my dear nurse, don't lie now—is he come, by your troth?

Nurse. Yes, by my truly, is he. *Miss Hoyd.* O Lord! I'll go and put on my laced tucker, though I'm locked up for a month for't.

[*Exeunt.* MISS HOYDEN *goes off capering, and twirling her doll by its leg.*]

ACT IV.

SCENE I. —*A Room in* SIR TUNBELLY CLUMSY'S *House.*

Enter MISS HOYDEN *and* NURSE.

Nurse. Well, miss, how do you like your husband that is to be?

Miss Hoyd. O Lord, nurse, I'm so overjoyed I can scarce contain myself!

Nurse. Oh, but you must have a care of being too fond; for men, nowadays, hate a woman that loves 'em.

Miss Hoyd. Love him! why, do you think I love him, nurse? Ecod I would not care if he was hanged, so I were but once married to him. No, that which pleases me is to think what work I'll make when I get to London; for when I am a wife and a lady both, ecod, I'll flaunt it with the best of 'em. Ay, and I shall have money enough to do so too, nurse.

Nurse. Ah, there's no knowing that, miss; for though these lords have a power of wealth indeed, yet, as I have heard say, they give it all to their sluts and their trulls, who joggle it about in their coaches, with a murrain to 'em, whilst poor madam sits sighing and wishing, and has not a spare half-crown to buy her a Practice of Piety.

Miss Hoyd. Oh, but for that, don't deceive yourself, nurse; for this I must say of my lord, he's as free as an open house at Christmas; for this very morning he told me I should have six hundred a year to buy pins. Now if he gives me six hundred a year to buy pins, what do you think he'll give me to buy petticoats?

Nurse. Ay, my dearest, he deceives thee foully, and he's no better than a rogue for his pains! These Londoners have got a gibberish with 'em would confound a gipsy. That which they call pin-money, is to buy everything in the versal world, down to their very shoe-knots. Nay, I have heard some folks say that some ladies, if they'll have gallants as they call 'em, are forced to find them out of their pin-money too. —But look, look, if his honour be not coming to you! —Now, if I were sure you would behave yourself handsomely, and not disgrace me that have brought you up, I'd leave you alone together.

Miss Hoyd. That's my best nurse; do as you'd be done by. Trust us together this once, and if I don't show my breeding, I wish I may never be married, but die an old maid.

Nurse. Well, this once I'll venture you. But if you disparage me—

Miss Hoyd. Never fear. [*Exit* NURSE.]

Enter TOM FASHION.

Fash. Your servant, madam; I'm glad to find you alone, for I have something of importance to speak to you about.

Miss Hoyd. Sir (my lord, I meant), you may speak to me about what you please, I shall give you a civil answer.

Fash. You give so obliging an one, it encourages me to tell you in a few words what I think, both for your interest and mine. Your father, I suppose you know, has resolved to make me happy in being your husband; and I hope I may obtain your consent to perform what he desires.

Miss Hoyd. Sir, I never disobey my father in anything but eating green gooseberries.

Fash. So good a daughter must needs be an admirable wife. I am therefore impatient till you are mine, and hope you will so far consider the violence of my love, that you won't have the cruelty to defer my happiness so long as your father designs it.

Miss Hoyd. Pray, my lord, how long is that?

Fash. Madam, a thousand years—a whole week.

Miss Hoyd. Why, I thought it was to be to-morrow morning, as soon as I was up. I'm sure nurse told me so.

Fash. And it shall be to-morrow morning, if you'll consent.

Miss Hoyd. If I'll consent! Why I thought I was to obey you as my husband.

Fash. That's when we are married. Till then, I'm to obey you.

Miss Hoyd. Why then, if we are to take it by turns, it's the same thing. I'll obey you now, and when we are married you shall obey me.

Fash. With all my heart. But I doubt we must get nurse on our side, or we shall hardly prevail with the chaplain.

Miss Hoyd. No more we shan't, indeed; for he loves her better than he loves his pulpit, and would always be a-preaching to her by his good will.

Fash. Why then, my dear, if you'll call her hither we'll persuade her presently.

Miss Hoyd. O Lud! I'll tell you a way how to persuade her to anything.

Fash. How's that?

Miss Hoyd. Why tell her she's a handsome comely woman, and give her half a crown.

Fash. Nay, if that will do, she shall have half a score of 'em.

Miss Hoyd. O gemini! for half that she'd marry you herself. —I'll run and call her. [*Exit.*]

Fash. So! matters go on swimmingly. This is a rare girl, i'faith. I shall have a fine time on't with her at London.

Enter LORY.

So, Lory, what's the matter?

Lory. Here, sir—an intercepted packet from the enemy; your brother's postilion brought it. I knew the livery, pretended to be a servant of Sir Tunbelly's, and so got possession of the letter.

Fash. [Looks at the letter.] Ouns! he tells Sir Tunbelly here that he will be with him this evening, with a large party to supper. —Egad, I must marry the girl directly.

Lory. Oh, zounds, sir, directly to be sure. Here she comes. *[Exit.]*

Fash. And the old Jezebel with her.

Re-enter MISS HOYDEN *and* NURSE How do you do, good Mrs. Nurse? I desired your young lady would give me leave to see you, that I might thank you for your extraordinary care and kind conduct in her education: pray accept this small acknowledgment for it at present, and depend upon my further kindness when I shall be that happy thing, her husband. *[Gives her money.]*

Nurse. [Aside.] Gold, by the maakins! — *[Aloud.]* Your honour's goodness is too great. Alas! all I can boast of is, I gave her pure and good milk, and so your honour would have said, an you had seen how the poor thing thrived, and how it would look up in my face, and crow and laugh, it would.

Miss Hoyd. [To NURSE, *taking her angrily aside.]* Pray, one word with you. Pr'ythee, nurse, don't stand ripping up old stories, to make one ashamed before one's love. Do you think such a fine proper gentleman as he is cares for a fiddlecome tale of a child? If you have a mind to make him have a good opinion of a woman, don't tell him what one did then, tell him what one can do now. —*[To* Tom FASHION. *]* I hope your honour will excuse my mis-manners to whisper before you. It was only to give some orders about the family.

Fash. Oh, everything, madam, is to give way to business; besides, good housewifery is a very commendable quality in a young lady.

Miss Hoyd. Pray, sir, are young ladies good housewives at London-town? Do they darn their own linen?

Fash. Oh no, they study how to spend money, not to save.

Miss Hoyd. Ecod, I don't know but that may be better sport, eh, nurse?

Fash. Well, you have your choice, when you come there.

Miss Hoyd. Shall I? then, by my troth, I'll get there as fast as I can. — [*To* NURSE.] His honour desires you'll be so kind as to let us be married to-morrow.

Nurse. To-morrow, my dear madam?

Fash. Ay, faith, nurse, you may well be surprised at miss's wanting to put it off so long. To-morrow! no, no; 'tis now, this very hour, I would have the ceremony performed.

Miss Hoyd. Ecod, with all my heart.

Nurse. O mercy! worse and worse!

Fash. Yes, sweet nurse, now and privately; for all things being signed and sealed, why should Sir Tunbelly make us stay a week for a wedding-dinner?

Nurse. But if you should be married now, what will you do when Sir Tunbelly calls for you to be married?

Miss Hoyd. Why then we will be married again.

Nurse. What twice, my child?

Miss Hoyd. Ecod, I don't care how often I'm married, not I.

Nurse. Well, I'm such a tender-hearted fool, I find I can refuse you nothing. So you shall e'en follow your own inventions. *Miss Hoyd.* Shall I? O Lord, I could leap over the moon!

Fash. Dear nurse, this goodness of yours shall be still more rewarded. But now you must employ your power with the chaplain, that he may do this friendly office too, and then we shall be all happy. Do you think you can prevail with him?

Nurse. Prevail with him! or he shall never prevail with me, I can tell him that.

Fash. I'm glad to hear it; however, to strengthen your interest with him, you may let him know I have several fat livings in my gift, and that the first that falls shall be in your disposal.

Nurse. Nay, then, I'll make him marry more folks than one, I'll promise him!

Miss Hoyd. Faith, do, nurse, make him marry you too; I'm sure he'll do't for a fat living.

Fash. Well, nurse, while you go and settle matters with him, your lady and I will go and take a walk in the garden. — [*Exit* NURSE.] Come, madam, dare you venture yourself alone with me? [*Takes* MISS HOYDEN *by the hand.]*

Miss Hoyd. Oh dear, yes, sir; I don't think you'll do anythink to me, I need be afraid on. [*Exeunt.]*

SCENE II. —AMANDA's *Dressing-room.*

Enter AMANDA *followed by her* MAID.

Maid. If you please, madam, only to say whether you'll have me buy them or not?

Aman. Yes—no—Go, teaser; I care not what you do. Pr'ythee, leave me. [*Exit* MAID.]

Enter BERINTHIA.

Ber. What, in the name of Jove, is the matter with you?

Aman. The matter, Berinthia! I'm almost mad; I'm plagued to death.

Ber. Who is it that plagues you?

Aman. Who do you think should plague a wife but her husband?

Ber. O, ho! is it come to that? —We shall have you wish yourself a widow, by-and-by.

Aman. Would I were anything but what I am! A base, ungrateful man, to use me thus!

Ber. What, has he given you fresh reason to suspect his wandering?

Aman. Every hour gives me reason.

Ber. And yet, Amanda, you perhaps at this moment cause in another's breast the same tormenting doubts and jealousies which you feel so sensibly yourself.

Aman. Heaven knows I would not.

Ber. Why, you can't tell but there may be some one as tenderly attached to Townly, whom you boast of as your conquest, as you can be to your husband?

Aman. I'm sure, I never encouraged his pretensions.

Ber. Psha! psha! no sensible man ever perseveres to love without encouragement. Why have you not treated him as you have Lord Foppington?

Aman. Because he presumed not so far. But let us drop the subject. Men, not women, are riddles. Mr. Loveless now follows some flirt for variety, whom I'm sure he does not like so well as he does me.

Ber. That's more than you know, madam.

Aman. Why, do you know the ugly thing?

Ber. I think I can guess at the person; but she's no such ugly thing neither.

Aman. Is she very handsome?

Ber. Truly I think so.

Aman. Whate'er she be, I'm sure he does not like her well enough to bestow anything more than a little outward gallantry upon her.

Ber. [*Aside.*] Outward gallantry! I can't bear this. — [*Aloud.*] Come, come, don't you be too secure, Amanda: while you suffer Townly to imagine that you do not detest him for his designs on you, you have no right to complain that your husband is engaged elsewhere. But here comes the person we were speaking of.

Enter COLONEL TOWNLY.

Col. Town. Ladies, as I come uninvited, I beg, if I intrude, you will use the same freedom in turning me out again.

Aman. I believe it is near the time Loveless said he would be at home. He talked of accepting Lord Foppington's invitation to sup at Sir Tunbelly Clumsy's.

Col. Town. His lordship has done me the honour to invite me also. If you'll let me escort you, I'll let you into a mystery as we go, in which you must play a part when we arrive.

Aman. But we have two hours yet to spare; the carriages are not ordered till eight, and it is not a five minutes' drive. So, cousin, let us keep the colonel to play at piquet with us, till Mr. Loveless comes home.

Ber. As you please, madam; but you know I have a letter to write.

Col. Town. Madam, you know you may command me, though I am a very wretched gamester.

Aman. Oh, you play well enough to lose your money, and that's all the ladies require; and so, without any more ceremony, let us go into the next room, and call for cards and candles.

[*Exeunt.*]

SCENE III. —BERINTHIA'S *Dressing-room.*

Enter LOVELESS.

Love. So, thus far all's well: I have got into her dressing-room, and it being dusk, I think nobody has perceived me steal into the house. I heard Berinthia tell my wife she had some particular letters to write this evening, before she went to Sir Tunbelly's, and here are the implements of correspondence. —Howshall I muster up assurance to show myself, when she comes? I think she has given me encouragement; and, to do my impudence justice, I have made the most of it. —I hear a door open, and some one coming. If it should be my wife, what the devil should I say? I believe she mistrusts me, and, by my life, I don't deserve her tenderness. However, I am determined to reform, though not yet. Ha! Berinthia! —So, I'll step in here, till I see what sort of humour she is in. [*Goes into the closet.*]

Enter BERINTHIA.

Ber. Was ever so provoking a situation! To think I should sit and hear him compliment Amanda to my face! I have lost all patience with them both! I would not for something have Loveless know what temper of mind they have piqued me into; yet I can't bear to leave them together. No, I'll put my papers away, and return, to disappoint them. —[*Goes to the closet.*]—O Lord! a ghost! a ghost! a ghost!

Re-enter LOVELESS.

Love. Peace, my angel; it's no ghost, but one worth a hundred spirits.

Ber. How, sir, have you had the insolence to presume to— run in again; here's somebody coming. [LOVELESS *goes into the closet.*]

Enter MAID.

Maid. O Lord, ma'am, what's the matter?

Ber. O Heavens! I'm almost frightened out of my wits! I thought verily I had seen a ghost, and 'twas nothing but a black hood pinned against the wall. You may go again; I am the fearfullest fool! [Exit MAID.]

Re-enter LOVELESS.

Love. Is the coast clear?

Ber. The coast clear! Upon my word, I wonder at your assurance.

Love. Why, then, you wonder before I have given you a proof of it. But where's my wife?

Ber. At cards.

Love. With whom?

Ber. With Townly.

Love. Then we are safe enough.

Ber. You are so! Some husbands would be of another mind were he at cards with their wives.

Love. And they'd be in the right on't, too; but I dare

trust mine.

Ber. Indeed! and she, I doubt not, has the same confidence in you. Yet, do you think she'd be content to come and find you here?

Love. Egad, as you say, that's true! —Then for fear she should come, hadn't we better go into the next room, out of her way?

Ber. What, in the dark?

Love. Ay, or with a light, which you please.

Ber. You are certainly very impudent.

Love. Nay, then—let me conduct you, my angel!

Ber. Hold, hold! you are mistaken in your angel, I assure you.

Love. I hope not; for by this hand I swear—

Ber. Come, come, let go my hand, or I shall hate you! — I'll cry out, as I live!

Love. Impossible! you cannot be so cruel.

Ber. Ha! here's some one coming. Begone instantly.

Love. Will you promise to return, if I remain here?

Ber. Never trust myself in a room again with you while I live.

Love. But I have something particular to communicate to you.

Ber. Well, well, before we go to Sir Tunbelly's, I'll walk

upon the lawn. If you are fond of a moonlight evening, you'll find me there.

Love. I'faith, they're coming here now! I take you at your word. [*Exit into the closet.*]

Ber. 'Tis Amanda, as I live! I hope she has not heard his voice; though I mean she should have her share of jealousy in her turn.

Enter AMANDA.

Aman. Berinthia, why did you leave me?

Ber. I thought I only spoiled your party.

Aman. Since you have been gone, Townly has attempted to renew his importunities. I must break with him, for I cannot venture to acquaint Mr. Loveless with his conduct.

Ber. Oh, no! Mr. Loveless mustn't know of it by any means.

Aman. Oh, not for the world—I wish, Berinthia, you would undertake to speak to Townly on the subject.

Ber. Upon my word, it would be a very pleasant subject for me to talk upon! But, come, let us go back; and you may depend on't I'll not leave you together again, if I can help it.

[*Exeunt.*]

Re-enter LOVELESS.

Love. So—so! a pretty piece of business I have overheard! Townly makes love to my wife, and I am not to know it for all the world. I must inquire into this—and, by Heaven, if I find that Amanda has, in the smallest degree—yet what have I been at here! —Oh, 'sdeath! that's no rule. That wife alone unsullied credit wins, Whose virtues can atone her husband's sins, Thus, while the man has other nymphs in view, It suits the woman to be doubly true.

[*Exit.*]

ACT V.

SCENE I. —*The Garden behind* LOVELESS's *Lodgings.*

Enter LOVELESS.

Love. Now, does she mean to make a fool of me, or not! I shan't wait much longer, for my wife will soon be inquiring for me to set out on our supping party. Suspense is at all times the devil, but of all modes of suspense, the watching for a loitering mistress is the worst. —But let me accuse her no longer; she approaches with one smile to o'erpay the anxieties of a year.

Enter BERINTHIA.

O Berinthia, what a world of kindness are you in my debt! had you stayed five minutes longer—

Ber. You would have gone, I suppose?

Love. Egad, she's right enough. [*Aside.*]

Ber. And I assure you 'twas ten to one that I came at all. In short, I begin to think you are too dangerous a being to trifle with; and as I shall probably only make a fool of you at last, I believe we had better let matters rest as they are.

Love. You cannot mean it, sure?

Ber. What more would you have me give to a married man?

Love. How doubly cruel to remind me of my misfortunes!

Ber. A misfortune to be married to so charming a woman as Amanda?

Love. I grant her all her merit, but—'sdeath! now see what you have done by talking of her—she's here, by all that's unlucky, and Townly with her. —I'll observe them.

Ber. O Gad, we had better get out of the way; for I should feel as awkward to meet her as you.

Love. Ay, if I mistake not, I see Townly coming this way also. I must see a little into this matter. [*Steps aside.*]

Ber. Oh, if that's your intention, I am no woman if I suffer myself to be outdone in curiosity. [*Goes on the other side.*]

Enter AMANDA.

Aman. Mr. Loveless come home, and walking on the lawn! I will not suffer him to walk so late, though perhaps it is to show his neglect of me. —Mr. Loveless, I must speak with you. —Ha! Townly again! — How I am persecuted!

Enter COLONEL TOWNLY.

Col. Town. Madam, you seem disturbed.

Aman. Sir, I have reason.

Col. Town. Whatever be the cause, I would to Heaven it were in my power to bear the pain, or to remove the malady.

Aman. Your interference can only add to my distress.

Col. Town. Ah, madam, if it be the sting of unrequited love you suffer from, seek for your remedy in revenge: weigh well the strength and beauty of your charms, and rouse up that spirit a woman ought to bear. Disdain the false embraces of a husband. See at your feet a real lover; his zeal may give him title to your pity, although his merit cannot claim your love.

Love. So, so, very fine, i'faith! [*Aside.*]

Aman. Why do you presume to talk to me thus? Is this your friendship to Mr. Loveless? I perceive you will compel me at last to acquaint him with your treachery.

Col. Town. He could not upbraid me if you were. —He deserves it from me; for he has not been more false to you than faithless to me.

Aman. To you?

Col. Town. Yes, madam; the lady for whom he now deserts those charms which he was never worthy of, was mine by right; and, I imagine too, by inclination. Yes, madam, Berinthia, who now—

Aman. Berinthia! Impossible!

Col. Town. 'Tis true, or may I never merit your attention. She is the deceitful sorceress who now holds your husband's heart in bondage.

Aman. I will not believe it.

Col. Town. By the faith of a true lover, I speak from conviction. This very day I saw them together, and overheard—

Aman. Peace, sir! I will not even listen to such slander— this is a poor device to work on my resentment, to listen to your insidious addresses. No, sir; though Mr. Loveless may be capable of error, I am convinced I cannot be deceived so grossly in him as to believe what you now report; and for Berinthia, you should have fixed on some more probable person for my rival than her who is my relation and my friend: for while I am myself free from guilt, I will never believe that love can beget injury, or confidence create ingratitude.

Col. Town. If I do not prove to you—

Aman. You never shall have an opportunity. From the artful manner in which you first showed yourself to me, I might have been led, as far as virtue permitted, to have thought you less criminal than unhappy; but this last unmanly artifice merits at once my resentment and contempt. [*Exit.*]

Col. Town. Sure there's divinity about her; and she has dispensed some portion of honour's light to me: yet can I bear to lose Berinthia without revenge or compensation? Perhaps she is not so culpable as I thought her. I was mistaken when I began to think lightly of Amanda's virtue, and may be in my censure of my Berinthia. Surely

I love her still, for I feel I should be happy to find myself in the wrong. [*Exit.*]

Re-enter LOVELESS *and* BERINTHIA.

Ber. Your servant, Mr. Loveless.

Love. Your servant, madam.

Ber. Pray what do you think of this?

Love. Truly, I don't know what to say.

Ber. Don't you think we steal forth two contemptible creatures?

Love. Why, tolerably so, I must confess.

Ber. And do you conceive it possible for you ever to give Amanda the least uneasiness again?

Love. No, I think we never should indeed.

Ber. We! why, monster, you don't pretend that I ever entertained a thought?

Love. Why then, sincerely and honestly, Berinthia, there is something in my wife's conduct which strikes me so forcibly, that if it were not for shame, and the fear of hurting you in her opinion, I swear I would follow her, confess my error, and trust to her generosity for forgiveness.

Ber. Nay, pr'ythee, don't let your respect for me prevent you; for as my object in trifling with you was nothing more than to pique Townly, and as I perceive he has been actuated by a similar motive, you may depend on't I shall make no mystery of the matter to him.

Love. By no means inform him: for though I may choose to pass by his conduct without resentment, how will he presume to look me in the face again?

Ber. How will you presume to look him in the face again?

Love. He, who has dared to attempt the honour of my wife!

Ber. You who have dared to attempt the honour of his mistress! Come, come, be ruled by me, who affect more levity than I have, and don't think of anger in this cause. A readiness to resent injuries is a virtue only in those who are slow to injure.

Love. Then I will be ruled by you; and when you think proper to undeceive Townly, may your good qualities make as sincere a convert of him as Amanda's have of me. -When truth's extorted from us, then we own the robe of virtue is a sacred habit.Could women but our secret counsel scan— Could they but reach the deep reserve of man— To keep our love they'd rate their virtue high, They live together, and together die.

[*Exeunt.*]

SCENE II. —*A Room in* SIR TUNBELLY CLUMSY'S *House.*

Enter MISS HOYDEN, NURSE, *and* TOM FASHION.

Fash. This quick despatch of the chaplain's I take so kindly it shall give him claim to my favour as long as I live, I assure you.

Miss Hoyd. And to mine too, I promise you.

Nurse. I most humbly thank your honours; and may your children swarm about you like bees about a honeycomb!

Miss Hoyd. Ecod, with all my heart—the more the merrier, I say—ha, nurse?

Enter LORY.

Lory. One word with you, for Heaven's sake. [*Taking* TOM FASHION *hastily aside.*]

Fash. What the devil's the matter?

Lory. Sir, your fortune's ruined if you are not married. Yonder's your brother arrived, with two coaches and six horses, twenty footmen, and a coat worth fourscore pounds—so judge what will become of your lady's heart.

Fash. Is he in the house yet?

Lory. No, they are capitulating with him at the gate. Sir Tunbelly luckily takes him for an impostor; and I have told him that we have heard of this plot before.

Fash. That's right. —[*Turning to* MISS HOYDEN.] My dear, here's a troublesome business my man tells me of, but don't be frightened; we shall be too hard for the rogue. Here's an impudent fellow at the gate (not knowing I was come hither incognito) has taken my name upon him, in hopes to run away with you.

Miss Hoyd. Oh, the brazen-faced varlet! it's well we are married, or maybe we might never have been so.

Fash. [*Aside.*] Egad, like enough. —[*Aloud.*] Pr'ythee, nurse, run to Sir Tunbelly, and stop him from going to the gate before I speak to him.

Nurse. An't please your honour, my lady and I had better, lock ourselves up till the danger be over.

Fash. Do so, if you please.

Miss Hoyd. Not so fast; I won't be locked up any more, now I'm married.

Fash. Yes, pray, my dear, do, till we have seized this rascal.

Miss Hoyd. Nay, if you'll pray me, I'll do anything.

[*Exit with* NURSE.]

Fash. Hark you, sirrah, things are better than you imagine. The wedding's over.

Lory. The devil it is, sir! [*Capers about.*]

Fash. Not a word—all's safe—but Sir Tunbelly don't know it, nor must not yet. So I am resolved to brazen the brunt of the business out, and have the pleasure of turning the impostor upon his lordship, which I believe may easily be done.

Enter SIR TUNBELLY CLUMSY. Did you ever hear, sir, of so impudent an undertaking?

Sir Tun. Never, by the mass; but we'll tickle him, I'll warrant you.

Fash. They tell me, sir, he has a great many people with him, disguised like servants.

Sir Tun. Ay, ay, rogues enow, but we have mastered them. We only fired a few shot over their heads, and the regiment scoured in an instant. —Here, Tummus, bring in your prisoner.

Fash. If you please, Sir Tunbelly, it will be best for me not to confront this fellow yet, till you have heard how far his impudence will carry him.

Sir Tun. Egad, your lordship is an ingenious person. Your lordship, then, will please to step aside.

Lory. [*Aside.*] 'Fore heavens, I applaud my master's modesty! [*Exit with* TOM FASHION.]

Enter SERVANTS, *with* LORD FOPPINGTON *disarmed.*

Sir Tun. Come, bring him along, bring him along.

Lord Fop. What the plague do you mean, gentlemen? is it fair time, that you are all drunk before supper?

Sir Tun. Drunk, sirrah! here's an impudent rogue for you now. Drunk or sober, bully, I'm a justice o' the peace, and know how to deal with strollers.

Lord Fop. Strollers!

Sir Tun. Ay, strollers. Come, give an account of yourself. What's your name? where do you live? do you pay scot and lot? Come, are you a freeholder or a copyholder?

Lord Fop. And why dost thou ask me so many impertinent questions?

Sir Tun. Because I'll make you answer 'em, before I have done with you, you rascal, you!

Lord Fop. Before Gad, all the answer I can make to them is, that you are a very extraordinary old fellow, stap my vitals.

Sir Tun. Nay, if thou art joking deputy-lieutenants, we know how to deal with you. —Here, draw a warrant for him immediately.

Lord Fop. A warrant! What the devil is't thou wouldst be at, old gentleman?

Sir Tun. I would be at you, sirrah, (if my hands were not tied as a magistrate,) and with these two double fists beat your teeth down your throat, you dog, you! [*Driving him.*]

Lord Fop. And why wouldst thou spoil my face at that rate?

Sir Tun. For your design to rob me of my daughter, villain.

Lord Fop. Rob thee of thy daughter! Now do I begin to believe I am in bed and asleep, and that all this is but a dream. Pr'ythee, old father, wilt thou give me leave to ask thee one question?

Sir Tun. I can't tell whether I will or not, till I know what it is.

Lord Fop. Why, then, it is, whether thou didst not write to my Lord Foppington, to come down and marry thy daughter?

Sir Tun. Yes, marry, did I, and my Lord Foppington is come down, and shall marry my daughter before she's a day older.

Lord Fop. Now give me thy hand, old dad; I thought we should understand one another at last.

Sir Tun. The fellow's mad! —Here, bind him hand and foot.

[*They bind him.*]

Lord Fop. Nay, pr'ythee, knight, leave fooling; thy jest begins to grow dull.

Sir Tun. Bind him, I say—he's mad: bread and water, a dark room, and a whip, may bring him to his senses again.

Lord Fop. Pr'ythee, Sir Tunbelly, why should you take such an aversion to the freedom of my address as to suffer the rascals thus to skewer down my arms like a rabbit? —[*Aside.*] Egad, if I don't awake, by all that I can see, this is like to prove one of the most impertinent dreams that ever I dreamt in my life.

Re-enter MISS HOYDEN *and* NURSE.

Miss Hoyd. [*Going up to* LORD FOPPINGTON.] Is this he that would have run—Fough, how he stinks of sweets! —Pray, father, let him be dragged through the horse-pond.

Lord Fop. This must be my wife, by her natural inclination to her husband. [*Aside.*]

Miss Hoyd. Pray, father, what do you intend to do with him—hang him?

Sir Tun. That, at least, child.

Nurse. Ay, and it's e'en too good for him too.

Lord Fop. Madame la gouvernante, I presume: hitherto this appears to me to be one of the most extraordinary families that ever man of quality matched into. [*Aside.*]

Sir Tun. What's become of my lord, daughter?

Miss Hoyd. He's just coming, sir.

Lord Fop. My lord! what does he mean by that, now? [*Aside.*]

Re-enter TOM FASHION *and* LORY. Stap my vitals, Tam, now the dream's out! [*Runs.*]

Fash. Is this the fellow, sir, that designed to trick me of your daughter?

Sir Tun. This is he, my lord. How do you like him? Is not he a pretty fellow to get a fortune?

Fash. I find by his dress he thought your daughter might be taken with a beau.

Miss Hoyd. Oh, gemini! is this a beau? let me see him again. [*Surveys him.*] Ha! I find a beau is no such ugly thing, neither.

Fash. [*Aside.*] Egad, she'll be in love with him presently —I'll e'en have him sent away to jail. —[*To* LORD FOPPINGTON.] Sir, though your undertaking shows you a person of no extraordinary modesty, I suppose you ha'n't confidence enough to expect much favour from me?

Lord Fop. Strike me dumb, Tam, thou art a very impudent fellow.

Nurse. Look, if the varlet has not the effrontery to call his lordship plain Thomas!

Lord Fop. My Lord Foppington, shall I beg one word with your lordship?

Nurse. Ho, ho! it's my lord with him now! See how afflictions will humble folks.

Miss Hoyd. Pray, my lord—[*To* FASHION]—don't let him whisper too close, lest he bite your ear off.

Lord Fop. I am not altogether so hungry as your ladyship is pleased to imagine. —[*Aside to* TOM FASHION.] Look you, Tam, I am sensible I have not been so kind to you as I ought, but I hope you'll forgive what's past, and accept of the five thousand pounds I offer— thou mayst live in extreme splendour with it, stap my vitals!

Fash. It's a much easier matter to prevent a disease than to cure it. A quarter of that sum would have secured your mistress, twice as much cannot redeem her. [*Aside to* LORD FOPPINGTON.]

Sir Tun. Well, what says he?

Fash. Only the rascal offered me a bribe to let him go.

Sir Tun. Ay, he shall go, with a plague to him! —lead on, constable.

Enter SERVANT.

Ser. Sir, here is Muster Loveless, and Muster Colonel Townly, and some ladies to wait on you. [*To* TOM FASHION.]

Lory. [*Aside to* TOM FASHION.] So, sir, what will you do now?

Fash. [*Aside to* LORY.] Be quiet; they are in the plot. —[*Aloud.*] Only a few friends, Sir Tunbelly, whom I wish to introduce to you.

Lord Fop. Thou art the most impudent fellow, Tam, that ever nature yet brought into the world. —Sir Tunbelly, strike me speechless, but these are my friends and acquaintance, and my guests, and they will soon inform thee whether I am the true Lord Foppington or not.

Enter LOVELESS, COLONEL TOWNLY, AMANDA, *and* BERINTHIA. —LORD FOPPINGTON *accosts them as they pass, but none answer him.*

Fash. So, gentlemen, this is friendly; I rejoice to see you.

Col. Town. My lord, we are fortunate to be the witnesses of your lordship's happiness.

Love. But your lordship will do us the honour to introduce us to Sir Tunbelly Clumsy?

Aman. And us to your lady.

Lord Fop. Gad take me, but they are all in a story! [*Aside.*]

Sir Tun. Gentlemen, you do me much honour; my Lord Foppington's friends will ever be welcome to me and mine.

Fash. My love, let me introduce you to these ladies.

Miss Hoyd. By goles, they look so fine and so stiff, I am almost ashamed to come nigh 'em.

Aman. A most engaging lady indeed!

Miss Hoyd. Thank ye, ma'am.

Ber. And I doubt not will soon distinguish herself in the beau monde.

Miss Hoyd. Where is that?

Fash. You'll soon learn, my dear.

Love. But Lord Foppington—

Lord Fop. Sir!

Love. Sir! I was not addressing myself to you, sir! —Pray who is this gentleman? He seems rather in a singular predicament—

Col. Town. For so well-dressed a person, a little oddly circumstanced, indeed.

Sir Tun. Ha! ha! ha! —So, these are your friends and your guests, ha, my adventurer?

Lord Fop. I am struck dumb with their impudence, and cannot positively say whether I shall ever speak again or not.

Sir Tun. Why, sir, this modest gentleman wanted to pass himself upon me as Lord Foppington, and carry off my daughter.

Love. A likely plot to succeed, truly, ha! ha!

Lord Fop. As Gad shall judge me, Loveless, I did not expect this from thee. Come, pr'ythee confess the joke; tell Sir Tunbelly that I am the real Lord Foppington, who yesterday made love to thy wife; was honoured by her with a slap on the face, and afterwards pinked through the body by thee.

Sir Tun. A likely story, truly, that a peer would behave thus.

Love. A pretty fellow, indeed, that would scandalize the character he wants to assume; but what will you do with him, Sir Tunbelly?

Sir Tun. Commit him, certainly, unless the bride and bridegroom choose to pardon him.

Lord Fop. Bride and bridegroom! For Gad's sake, Sir Tunbelly, 'tis tarture to me to hear you call 'em so.

Miss Hoyd. Why, you ugly thing, what would you have him call us—dog and cat?

Lord Fop. By no means, miss; for that sounds ten times more like man and wife than t'other.

Sir Tun. A precious rogue this to come a-wooing!

Re-enter SERVANT.

Ser. There are some gentlefolks below to wait upon Lord Foppington. [*Exit.*]

Col. Town. 'Sdeath, Tom, what will you do now? [*Aside to* TOM FASHION.]

Lord Fop. Now, Sir Tunbelly, here are witnesses who I believe are not corrupted.

Sir Tun. Peace, fellow! —Would your lordship choose to have your guests shown here, or shall they wait till we come to 'em?

Fash. I believe, Sir Tunbelly, we had better not have these visitors here yet. —[*Aside.*] Egad, all must out.

Love. Confess, confess; we'll stand by you. [*Aside to* TOM FASHION.]

Lord Fop. Nay, Sir Tunbelly, I insist on your calling evidence on both sides—and if I do not prove that fellow an impostor—

Fash. Brother, I will save you the trouble, by now confessing that I am not what I have passed myself for. —Sir Tunbelly, I am a gentleman, and I flatter myself a man of character; but'tis with great pride I assure you I am not Lord Foppington.

Sir Tun. Ouns! —what's this? —an impostor? —a cheat? —fire and faggots, sir, if you are not Lord Foppington, who the devil are you?

Fash. Sir, the best of my condition is, I am your son-in-law; and the worst of it is, I am brother to that noble peer.

Lord Fop. Impudent to the last, Gad dem me!

Sir Tun. My son-in-law! not yet, I hope.

Fash. Pardon me, sir; thanks to the goodness of your chaplain, and the kind offices of this gentlewoman.

Lory. 'Tis true indeed, sir; I gave your daughter away, and Mrs. Nurse, here, was clerk.

Sir Tun. Knock that rascal down! —But speak, Jezebel, how's this?

Nurse. Alas! your honour, forgive me; I have been overreached in this business as well as you. Your worship knows, if the wedding-dinner had been ready, you would have given her away with your own hands.

Sir Tun. But how durst you do this without acquainting me?

Nurse. Alas! if your worship had seen how the poor thing begged and prayed, and clung and twined about me like ivy round an old wall, you would say, I who had nursed it, and reared it, must have had a heart like stone to refuse it.

Sir Tun. Ouns! I shall go mad! Unloose my lord there, you scoundrels!

Lord Fop. Why, when these gentlemen are at leisure, I should be glad to congratulate you on your son-in-law, with a little more freedom of address.

Miss Hoyd. Egad, though, I don't see which is to be my husband after all.

Love. Come, come, Sir Tunbelly, a man of your understanding must perceive that an affair of this kind is not to be mended by anger and reproaches.

Col. Town. Take my word for it, Sir Tunbelly, you are only tricked into a son-in-law you may be proud of: my friend Tom Fashion is as honest a fellow as ever breathed.

Love. That he is, depend on't; and will hunt or drink with you most affectionately: be generous, old boy, and forgive them—

Sir Tun. Never! the hussy! —when I had set my heart on getting her a title.

Lord Fop. Now, Sir Tunbelly, that I am untrussed—give me leave to thank thee for the very extraordinary reception I have met with in thy damned, execrable mansion; and at the same time to assure you, that of all the bumpkins and blockheads I have had the misfortune to meek with, thou art the most obstinate and egregious, strike me ugly!

Sir Tun. What's this! I believe you are both rogues alike.

Lord Fop. No, Sir Tunbelly, thou wilt find to thy unspeakable mortification, that I am the real Lord Foppington, who was to have disgraced myself by an alliance with a clod; and that thou hast matched thy girl to a beggarly younger brother of mine, whose title deeds might be contained in thy tobacco-box.

Sir Tun. Puppy! puppy! —I might prevent their being beggars, if I chose it; for I could give 'em as good a rent-roll as your lordship.

Lord Fop. Ay, old fellow, but you will not do that—for that would be acting like a Christian, and thou art a barbarian, stap my vitals.

Sir Tun. Udzookers! now six such words more, and I'll forgive them directly.

Love. 'Slife, Sir Tunbelly, you should do it, and bless yourself— Ladies, what say you?

Aman. Good Sir Tunbelly, you must consent.

Ber. Come, you have been young yourself, Sir Tunbelly.

Sir Tun. Well then, if I must, I must; but turn—turn that sneering lord out, however, and let me be revenged on somebody. But first look whether I am a barbarian or not; there, children, I join your hands; and when I'm in a better humour, I'll give you my blessing.

Love. Nobly done, Sir Tunbelly! and we shall see you dance at a grandson's christening yet.

Miss Hoyd. By goles, though, I don't understand this! What! an't I to be a lady after all? only plain Mrs. —What's my husband's name, nurse?

Nurse. Squire Fashion.

Miss Hoyd. Squire, is he? —Well, that's better than nothing.

Lord Fop. [*Aside.*] Now I will put on a philosophic air, and show these people, that it is not possible to put a man of my quality out of countenance. —[*Aloud.*] Dear Tam, since things are fallen out, pr'ythee give me leave to wish thee joy; I do it *de bon coeur*, strike me dumb! You have married into a family of great politeness and uncommon elegance of manners, and your bride appears to be a lady beautiful in person, modest in her deportment, refined in her sentiments, and of nice morality, split my windpipe!

Miss Hoyd. By goles, husband, break his bones if he calls me names!

Fash. Your lordship may keep up your spirits with your grimace, if you please; I shall support mine, by Sir Tunbelly's favour, with this lady and three thousand pounds a year.

Lord Fop. Well, adieu, Tam! —Ladies, I kiss your, hands! — Sir Tunbelly, I shall now quit this thy den; but while I retain the use of my arms, I shall ever remember thou art a demned horrid savage; Ged demn me! [*Exit.*]

Sir Tun. By the mass, 'tis well he's gone—for I should ha' been provoked, by-and-by, to ha' dun un a mischief. Well, if this is a lord, I think Hoyden has luck on her side, in troth.

Col. Town. She has, indeed, Sir Tunbelly. —But I hear the fiddles; his lordship, I know, has provided 'em.

Love. Oh, a dance and a bottle, Sir Tunbelly, by all means!

Sir Tun. I had forgot the company below; well—what—we must be merry, then, ha? and dance and drink, ha? Well, 'fore George, you shan't say I do these things by halves. Son-in-law there looks like a hearty rogue, so we'll have a night on't: and which of these ladies will be the old man's partner, ha? —Ecod, I don't know how I came to be in so good a humour.

Ber. Well, Sir Tunbelly, my friend and I both will endeavour to keep you so: you have done a generous action, and are entitled to our attention. If you should be at a loss to divert your new guests, we will assist you to relate to them the plot of your daughter's marriage, and his lordship's deserved mortification; a subject which perhaps may afford no bad evening's entertainment.

Sir Tun. Ecod, with all my heart; though I am a main bungler at a long story.

Ber. Never fear; we will assist you, if the tale is judged worth being repeated; but of this you may be assured, that while the intention is evidently to please, British auditors will ever be indulgent to the errors of the performance. [Exeunt omnes.]

THE CRITIC;

OR, A TRAGEDY REHEARSED *A DRAMATIC PIECE IN THREE ACTS*

TO MRS. GREVILLE

MADAM, — In requesting your permission to address the following pages to you, which, as they aim themselves to be critical, require every protection and allowance that approving taste or friendly prejudice can give them, I yet ventured to mention no other motive than the gratification of private friendship and esteem. Had I suggested a hope that your implied approbation would give a sanction to their defects, your particular reserve, and dislike to the reputation of critical taste, as well as of poetical talent, would have made you refuse the protection of your name to such a purpose. However, I am not so ungrateful as now to attempt to combat this disposition in you. I shall not here presume to argue that the present state of poetry claims and expects every assistance that taste and example can afford it; nor endeavour to prove that a fastidious concealment of the most elegant productions of judgment and fancy is an ill return for the possession of those endowments. Continue to deceive yourself in the idea that you are known only to be eminently admired and regarded for the valuable qualities that attach private friendships, and the graceful talents that adorn conversation. Enough of what you have written has stolen into full public notice to answer my purpose; and you will, perhaps, be the only person, conversant in elegant literature, who shall read this address and not perceive that by publishing your particular approbation of the following drama, I have a more interested object than to boast the true respect and regard with which I have the honour to be, Madam, your very sincere and obedient humble servant, R. B. SHERIDAN.

DRAMATIS PERSONAE

AS ORIGINALLY ACTED AT DRURY LANE THEATRE IN 1779

SIR FRETFUL PLAGIARY. *Mr. Parsons.*

PUFF. *Mr. King.*

DANGLE. *Mr. Dodd*

SNEER. *Mr. Palmer.*

SIGNOR PASTICCIO RITORNELLO. *Mr. Delpini.*

INTERPRETER. *Mr. Baddeley.*

UNDER PROMPTER. *Mr. Phillimore.*

MR. HOPKINS. *Mr. Hopkins.*

MRS. DANGLE. *Mrs. Hopkins.*

SIGNORE PASTICCIO RITORNELLO. *Miss Field and the Miss Abrams.*

Scenemen, Musicians, *and* Servants.

CHARACTERS OF THE TRAGEDY

LORD BURLEIGH. *Mr. Moody.*

GOVERNOR OF TILBURY FORT. *Mr. Wrighten.*

EARL OF LEICESTER. *Mr. Farren.*

SIR WALTER RALEIGH. *Mr. Burton.*

SIR CHRISTOPHER HATTON. *Mr. Waldron.*

MASTER OF THE HORSE. *Mr. Kenny.*

DON FEROLO WHISKERANDOS. *Mr. Bannister, jun.*

BEEFEATER. *Mr. Wright.*

JUSTICE. *Mr. Packer.*

SON. *Mr. Lamash.*

CONSTABLE. *Mr. Fawcett.*

THAMES. *Mr. Gawdry.*

TILBURINA. *Miss Pope.*

CONFIDANT. *Mrs. Bradshaw.*

JUSTICE's LADY. *Mrs. Johnston.*

FIRST NIECE. *Miss Collett.*

SECOND NIECE. *Miss Kirby.*

Knights, Guards, Constables, Sentinels, Servants, Chorus, Rivers, Attendants, &c., &c.

SCENE—LONDON: *in* DANGLES *House during the First Act,*

and throughout the rest of the Play in DRURY LANE THEATRE.

PROLOGUE

BY THE HONOURABLE RICHARD FITZPATRICK

THE sister Muses, whom these realms obey,
Who o'er the drama hold divided sway,
Sometimes by evil counsellors, 'tis said,
Like earth-born potentates have been misled.
In those gay days of wickedness and wit,
When Villiers criticised what Dryden writ,
The tragic queen, to please a tasteless crowd,
Had learn'd to bellow, rant, and roar so loud,
That frighten'd Nature, her best friend before,
The blustering beldam's company foreswore;
Her comic sister, who had wit 'tis true,
With all her merits, had her failings too:
And would sometimes in mirthful moments use
A style too flippant for a well-bred muse;
Then female modesty abash'd began
To seek the friendly refuge of the fan,
Awhile behind that slight intrenchment stood,
Till driven from thence, she left the stage for good.
In our more pious, and far chaster times,
These sure no longer are the Muse's crimes!
But some complain that, former faults to shun,
The reformation to extremes has run.
The frantic hero's wild delirium past,
Now insipidity succeeds bombast:
So slow Melpomene's cold numbers creep,
Here dulness seems her drowsy court to keep,
And we are scarce awake, whilst you are fast asleep.
Thalia, once so ill-behaved and rude,
Reform'd, is now become an arrant prude;
Retailing nightly to the yawning pit
The purest morals, undefiled by wit!
Our author offers, in these motley scenes,
A slight remonstrance to the drama's queens:
Nor let the goddesses be over nice;
Free-spoken subjects give the best advice.
Although not quite a novice in his trade,
His cause to-night requires no common aid.
To this, a friendly, just, and powerful court,

I come ambassador to beg support.
Can he undaunted brave the critic's rage?
In civil broils with brother bards engage?
Hold forth their errors to the public eye,
Nay more, e'en newspapers themselves defy?
Say, must his single arm encounter all?
By number vanquish'd, e'en the brave may fall;
And though no leader should success distrust,
Whose troops are willing, and whose cause is just;
To bid such hosts of angry foes defiance,
His chief dependence must be, your alliance.

ACT I.

SCENE I. —*A Room in* DANGLE's *House.*

Mr. *and* MRS. DANGLE *discovered at breakfast, and reading newspapers.*

Dang. [*Reading.*] *Brutus to Lord North.* —*Letter the second on the State of the Army*—Psha! *To the first L dash D of the A dash Y.* —*Genuine extract of a Letter from St. Kitt's.* —*Coxheath*

Intelligence. —*It is now confidently asserted that Sir Charles*

Hardy—Psha! nothing but about the fleet and the nation! —and

I hate all politics but theatrical politics. —Where's the Morning

Chronicle?

Mrs. Dang. Yes, that's your Gazette.

Dang. So, here we have it. —[*Reads.*] *Theatrical intelligence extraordinary.* —*We hear there is a new tragedy in rehearsal at Drury Lane Theatre, called the Spanish Armada, said to be written by Mr. Puff, a gentleman well-known in the theatrical world. If we may allow ourselves to give credit to the report of the performers, who, truth to say, are in general but indifferent judges, this piece abounds with the most striking and received beauties of modern composition.* —So! I am very glad my friend Puff's tragedy is in such forwardness. —Mrs. Dangle, my dear, you will be very glad to hear that Puff's tragedy—

Mrs. Dang. Lord, Mr. Dangle, why will you plague me abou such nonsense? —Now the plays are begun I shall have no peace. — Isn't it sufficient to make yourself ridiculous by your passion for the theatre, without continually teasing me to join you? Why can't you ride your hobby-horse without desiring to place me on a pillion behind you, Mr. Dangle?

Dang. Nay, my dear, I was only going to read—

Mrs. Dang. No, no; you will never read anything that's worth listening to. You hate to hear about your country; there are letters every day with Roman signatures, demonstrating the certainty of an invasion, and proving that the nation is utterly undone. But you never will read anything to entertain one.*Dang.* What has a woman to do with politics, Mrs. Dangle?

Mrs. Dang. And what have you to do with the theatre, Mr. Dangle? Why should you affect the character of a critic? I have no patience with you! —haven't you made yourself the jest of all your acquaintance by your interference in matters where you have no business? Are you not called a theatrical Quidnunc, and a mock Maecenas to second-hand authors?

Dang. True; my power with the managers is pretty notorious. But is it no credit to have applications from all quarters for my interest— from lords to recommend fiddlers, from ladies to get boxes, from authors to get answers, and from actors to get engagements?

Mrs. Dang. Yes, truly; you have contrived to get a share in all the plague and trouble of theatrical property, without the profit, or even the credit of the abuse that attends it.

Dang. I am sure, Mrs. Dangle, you are no loser by it, however; you have all the advantages of it. Mightn't you, last winter, have had the reading of the new pantomime a fortnight previous to its performance? And doesn't Mr. Fosbrook let you take places for a play before it is advertised, and set you down for a box for every new piece through the season? And didn't my friend, Mr. Smatter, dedicate his last farce to you at my particular request, Mrs. Dangle?

Mrs. Dang. Yes; but wasn't the farce damned, Mr. Dangle? And to be sure it is extremely pleasant to have one's house made the motley rendezvous of all the lackeys of literature; the very high 'Change of trading authors and jobbing critics! —Yes, my drawing-room is an absolute register-office for candidate actors, and poets without character. —Then to be continually alarmed with misses and ma'ams piping hysteric changes on Juliets and Dorindas, Pollys and Ophelias; and the very furniture trembling at the probationary starts and unprovoked rants of would-be Richards and Hamlets! —And what is worse than all, now that the manager has monopolized the Opera House, haven't we the signors and signoras calling here, sliding their smooth semibreves, and gargling glib divisions in their outlandish throats—with foreign emissaries and French spies, for aught I know, disguised like fiddlers and figure dancers?

Dang. Mercy! Mrs. Dangle!

Mrs. Dang. And to employ yourself so idly at such an alarming crisis as this too—when, if you had the least spirit, you would have been at the head of one of the Westminster associations—or trailing a volunteer pike in the Artillery Ground! But you—o' my conscience, I believe, if the French were landed to-morrow, your first inquiry would be, whether they had brought a theatrical troop with them.

Dang. Mrs. Dangle, it does not signify—I say the stage is *the mirror of Nature*, and the actors are *the Abstract and brief Chronicles of the Time*: and pray what can a man of sense study better? —Besides, you will not easily persuade me that there is no credit or importance in being at the head of a band of critics, who take upon them to decide for the whole town, whose opinion and patronage all writers solicit, and whose recommendation no manager dares refuse.

Mrs. Dang. Ridiculous! —Both managers and authors of the least merit laugh at your pretensions. —The public is their critic—without whose fair approbation they know no play can rest on the stage, and with whose applause they welcome such attacks as yours, and laugh at the malice of them, where they can't at the wit.

Dang. Very well, madam—very well!

Enter SERVANT.

Ser. Mr. Sneer, sir, to wait on you.

Dang. Oh, show Mr. Sneer up. —[*Exit* SERVANT.]— Plague on't, now we must appear loving and affectionate, or Sneer will hitch us into a story.

Mrs. Dang. With all my heart; you can't be more ridiculous than you are.

Dang. You are enough to provoke—

Enter SNEER.

Ha! my dear Sneer, I am vastly glad to see you. —My dear, here's Mr. Sneer.

Mrs. Dang. Good-morning to you, sir.

Dang. Mrs. Dangle and I have been diverting ourselves with the papers. Pray, Sneer, won't you go to Drury Lane Theatre the first night of Puff's tragedy?

Sneer. Yes; but I suppose one shan't be able to get in, for on the first night of a new piece they always fill the house with orders to support it. But here, Dangle, I have brought you two pieces, one of which you must exert yourself to make the managers accept, I can tell you that; for'tis written by a person of consequence.

Dang. So! now my plagues are beginning.

Sneer. Ay, I am glad of it, for now you'll be happy. Why, my dear Dangle, it is a pleasure to see how you enjoy your volunteer fatigue, and your solicited solicitations.

Dang. It's a great trouble—yet, egad, it's pleasant too. —Why, sometimes of a morning I have a dozen people call on me at breakfast-time, whose faces I never saw before, nor ever desire to see again.

Sneer. That must be very pleasant indeed!

Dang. And not a week but I receive fifty letters, and not a line in them about any business of my own.

Sneer. An amusing correspondence!

Dang. [*Reading.*] *Bursts into tears and exit.* —What, is this a tragedy?

Sneer. No, that's a genteel comedy, not a translation— only taken from the French: it is written in a style which they have lately tried to run down; the true sentimental, and nothing ridiculous in it from the beginning to the end.

Mrs. Dang. Well, if they had kept to that, I should not have been such an enemy to the stage; there was some edification to be got from those pieces, Mr. Sneer!

Sneer. I am quite of your opinion, Mrs. Dangle: the theatre, in proper hands, might certainly be made the school of morality; but now, I am sorry to say it, people seem to go there principally for their entertainment!

Mrs. Dang. It would have been more to the credit of the managers to have kept it in the other line.

Sneer. Undoubtedly, madam; and hereafter perhaps to have had it recorded, that in the midst of a luxurious and dissipated age, they preserved two houses in the capital, where the conversation was always moral at least, if not entertaining!

Dang. Now, egad, I think the worst alteration is in the nicety of the audience! —No *double-entendre*, no smart innuendo admitted; even Vanbrugh and Congreve obliged to undergo a bungling reformation!

Sneer. Yes, and our prudery in this respect is just on a par with the artificial bashfulness of a courtesan, who increases the blush upon her cheek in an exact proportion to the diminution of her modesty.

Dang. Sneer can't even give the public a good word! But what have we here? —This seems a very odd—

Sneer. Oh, that's a comedy on a very new plan; replete with wit and mirth, yet of a most serious moral! You see it is called *The Reformed House-breaker*; where, by the mere force of humour, house-breaking is put in so ridiculous a light, that if the piece has its proper run, I have no doubt but that bolts and bars will be entirely useless by the end of the season.

Dang. Egad, this is new indeed!

Sneer. Yes; it is written by a particular friend of mine, who has discovered that the follies and foibles of society are subjects unworthy the notice of the comic muse, who should be taught to stoop only to the greater vices and blacker crimes of humanity— gibbeting capital offences in five acts, and pillorying petty larcenies in two. — In short, his idea is to dramatize the penal laws, and make the stage a court of ease to the Old Bailey.

Dang. It is truly moral.

Re-enter SERVANT.

Ser. Sir Fretful Plagiary, sir.

Dang. Beg him to walk up. — [*Exit* SERVANT.] Now, Mrs. Dangle, Sir Fretful Plagiary is an author to your own taste.

Mrs. Dang. I confess he is a favourite of mine, because everybody else abuses him.

Sneer. Very much to the credit of your charity, madam, if not of your judgment.

Dang. But, egad, he allows no merit to any author but himself, that's the truth on't — though he's my friend.

Sneer. Never. — He is as envious as an old maid verging on the desperation of six and thirty; and then the insidious humility with which he seduces you to give a free opinion on any of his works, can be exceeded only by the petulant arrogance with which he is sure to reject your observations.

Dang. Very true, egad — though he's my friend.

Sneer. Then his affected contempt of all newspaper strictures; though, at the same time, he is the sorest man alive, and shrinks like scorched parchment from the fiery ordeal of true criticism: yet he is so covetous of popularity, that he had rather be abused than not mentioned at all.

Dang. There's no denying it — though he is my friend.

Sneer. You have read the tragedy he has just finished, haven't you?

Dang. Oh, yes; he sent it to me yesterday.

Sneer. Well, and you think it execrable, don't you?

Dang. Why, between ourselves, egad, I must own—though he is my friend—that it is one of the most—He's here— [*Aside.*]—finished and most admirable perform—

Sir Fret. [*Without.*] Mr. Sneer with him did you say?

Enter SIR FRETFUL PLAGIARY.

Dang. Ah, my dear friend! —Egad, we were just speaking of your tragedy. —Admirable, Sir Fretful, admirable!

Sneer. You never did anything beyond it, Sir Fretful— never in your life.

Sir Fret. You make me extremely happy; for without a compliment, my dear Sneer, there isn't a man in the world whose judgment I value as I do yours and Mr. Dangle's.

Mrs. Dang. They are only laughing at you, Sir Fretful; for it was but just now that—

Dang. Mrs. Dangle! —Ah, Sir Fretful, you know Mrs. Dangle. —My friend Sneer was rallying just now: —he knows how she admires you, and—

Sir Fret. O Lord, I am sure Mr. Sneer has more taste and sincerity than to—[*Aside.*] A damned double-faced fellow!

Dang. Yes, yes—Sneer will jest—but a better humoured—

Sir Fret. Oh, I know—

Dang. He has a ready turn for ridicule—his wit costs him nothing.

Sir Fret. No, egad—or I should wonder how he came by it. [*Aside.*]

Mrs. Dang. Because his jest is always at the expense of his friend. [*Aside.*]

Dang. But, Sir Fretful, have you sent your play to the managers yet? —or can I be of any service to you?

Sir Fret. No, no, I thank you: I believe the piece had sufficient recommendation with it. —I thank you though. —I sent it to the manager of Covent Garden Theatre this morning.

Sneer. I should have thought now, that it might have been cast (as the actors call it) better at Drury Lane.

Sir Fret. O Lud! no—never send a play there while I live—hark'ee! [*Whispers* SNEER.]

Sneer. Writes himself! —I know he does.

Sir Fret. I say nothing—I take away from no man's merit—am hurt at no man's good fortune—I say nothing. —But this I will say— through all my knowledge of life, I have observed—that there is not a passion so strongly rooted in the human heart as envy.

Sneer. I believe you have reason for what you say, indeed.

Sir Fret. Besides—I can tell you it is not always so safe to leave a play in the hands of those who write themselves.

Sneer. What, they may steal from them, hey, my dear Plagiary?

Sir Fret. Steal! —to be sure they may; and, egad, serve your best thoughts as gypsies do stolen children, disfigure them to make 'em pass for their own.

Sneer. But your present work is a sacrifice to Melpomene, and he, you know, never—

Sir Fret. That's no security: a dexterous plagiarist may do anything. Why, sir, for aught I know, he might take out some of the best things in my tragedy, and put them into his own comedy.

Sneer. That might be done, I dare be sworn.

Sir Fret. And then, if such a person gives you the least hint or assistance, he is devilish apt to take the merit of the whole—

Dang. If it succeeds.

Sir Fret. Ay, but with regard to this piece, I think I can hit that gentleman, for I can safely swear he never read it.

Sneer. I'll tell you how you may hurt him more.

Sir Fret. How?

Sneer. Swear he wrote it.

Sir Fret. Plague on't now, Sneer, I shall take it ill! —I believe you want to take away my character as an author.

Sneer. Then I am sure you ought to be very much obliged to me.

Sir Fret. Hey! —sir! —

Dang. Oh, you know, he never means what he says.

Sir Fret. Sincerely then—do you like the piece?

Sneer. Wonderfully!

Sir Fret. But come, now, there must be something that you think might be mended, hey? —Mr. Dangle, has nothing struck you?

Dang. Why, faith, it is but an ungracious thing for the most part, to—

Sir Fret. With most authors it is just so, indeed; they are in general strangely tenacious! But, for my part, I am never so well pleased as when a judicious critic points out any defect to me; for what is the purpose of showing a work to a friend, if you don't mean to profit by his opinion?

Sneer. Very true. —Why, then, though I seriously admire the piece upon the whole, yet there is one small objection; which, if you'll give me leave, I'll mention.

Sir Fret. Sir, you can't oblige me more.

Sneer. I think it wants incident.

Sir Fret. Good God! you surprise me! —wants incident!

Sneer. Yes; I own I think the incidents are too few.

Sir Fret. Good God! Believe me, Mr. Sneer, there is no person for whose judgment I have a more implicit deference. But I protest to you, Mr. Sneer, I am only apprehensive that the incidents are too crowded. —My dear Dangle, how does it strike you?

Dang. Really I can't agree with my friend Sneer. I think the plot quite sufficient; and the four first acts by many degrees the best I ever read or saw in my life. If, I might venture to suggest anything, it is that the interest rather falls off in the fifth.

Sir Fret. Rises, I believe you mean, sir.

Dang. No, I don't, upon my word.

Sir Fret. Yes, yes, you do, upon my soul! —it certainly don't fall off, I assure you. —No, no; it don't fall off.

Dang. Now, Mrs. Dangle, didn't you say it struck you in the same light?

Mrs. Dang. No, indeed, I did not. —I did not see a fault in any part of the play, from the beginning to the end.

Sir Fret. Upon my soul, the women are the best judges after all!

Mrs. Dang. Or, if I made any objection, I am sure it was to nothing in the piece; but that I was afraid it was on the whole, a little too long.

Sir Fret. Pray, madam, do you speak as to duration of time; or do you mean that the story is tediously spun out?

Mrs. Dang. O Lud! no. —I speak only with reference to the usual length of acting plays.

Sir Fret. Then I am very happy—very happy indeed— because the play is a short play, a remarkably short play. I should not venture to differ with a lady on a point of taste; but on these occasions, the watch, you know, is the critic.

Mrs. Dang. Then, I suppose, it must have been Mr. Dangle's drawling manner of reading it to me.

Sir Fret. Oh, if Mr. Dangle read it, that's quite another affair! —But I assure you, Mrs. Dangle, the first evening you can spare me three hours and a half, I'll undertake to read you the whole, from beginning to end, with the prologue and epilogue, and allow time for the music between the acts.

Mrs. Dang. I hope to see it on the stage next.

Dang. Well, Sir Fretful, I wish you may be able to get rid as easily of the newspaper criticisms as you do of ours.

Sir Fret. The newspapers! Sir, they are the most villainous— licentious—abominable—infernal. —Not that I ever read them— no—I make it a rule never to look into a newspaper.

Dang. You are quite right; for it certainly must hurt an author of delicate feelings to see the liberties they take.

Sir Fret. No, quite the contrary! their abuse is, in fact, the best panegyric—I like it of all things. An author's reputation is only in danger from their support.

Sneer. Why, that's true—and that attack, now, on you the other day—

Sir Fret. What? where?

Dang. Ay, you mean in a paper of Thursday: it was completely ill-natured, to be sure.

Sir Fret. Oh so much the better. —Ha! Ha! Ha! I wouldn't have it otherwise.

Dang. Certainly it is only to be laughed at; for—

Sir Fret. You don't happen to recollect what the fellow said, do you?

Sneer. Pray, Dangle—Sir Fretful seems a little anxious—

Sir Fret. O Lud, no! —anxious! —not I—not the least. — I—but one may as well hear, you know.

Dang. Sneer, do you recollect? —[*Aside to* SNEER.] Make out something.

Sneer. [*Aside to* DANGLE.] I will. —[*Aloud.*] Yes, yes, I remember perfectly.

Sir Fret. Well, and pray now—not that it signifies—what might the gentleman say?

Sneer. Why, he roundly asserts that you have not the slightest invention or original genius whatever; though you are the greatest traducer of all other authors living.

Sir Fret. Ha! ha! ha! —very good!

Sneer. That as to comedy, you have not one idea of your own, he believes, even in your commonplace-book—where stray jokes and pilfered witticisms are kept with as much method as the ledger of the lost and stolen office.

Sir Fret. Ha! ha! ha! —very pleasant!

Sneer. Nay, that you are so unlucky as not to have the skill even to steal with taste: —but that you glean from the refuse of obscure volumes, where more judicious plagiarists have been before you; so that the body of your work is a composition of dregs and sentiments—like a bad tavern's worst wine.

Sir Fret. Ha! ha!

Sneer. In your more serious efforts, he says, your bombast would be less intolerable, if the thoughts were ever suited to the expression;

but the homeliness of the sentiment stares through the fantastic encumbrance of its fine language, like a clown in one of the new uniforms!

Sir Fret. Ha! ha!

Sneer. That your occasional tropes and flowers suit the general coarseness of your style, as tambour sprigs would a ground of linsey-woolsey; while your imitations of Shakspeare resemble the mimicry of Falstaff's page, and are about as near the standard as the original.

Sir Fret. Ha!

Sneer. In short, that even the finest passages you steal are of no service to you; for the poverty of your own language prevents their assimilating; so that they lie on the surface like lumps of marl on a barren moor, encumbering what it is not in their power to fertilize!

Sir Fret. [*After great agitation.*] Now, another person would be vexed at this!

Sneer. Oh! but I wouldn't have told you—only to divert you.

Sir Fret. I know it—I am diverted. —Ha! ha! ha! —not the least invention! —Ha! ha! ha! —very good! —very good!

Sneer. Yes—no genius! ha! ha! ha!

Dang. A severe rogue! ha! ha! ha! But you are quite right, Sir Fretful, never to read such nonsense.

Sir Fret. To be sure—for if there is anything to one's praise, it is a foolish vanity to be gratified at it; and, if it is abuse—why one is always sure to hear of it from one damned good-natured friend or other!

Enter SERVANT.

Ser. Sir, there is an Italian gentleman, with a French interpreter, and three young ladies, and a dozen musicians, who say they are sent by Lady Rondeau and Mrs. Fugue.

Dang. Gadso! they come by appointment! —Dear Mrs. Dangle, do let them know I'll see them directly.

Mrs. Dang. You know, Mr. Dangle, I shan't understand a word they say.

Dang. But you hear there's an interpreter.

Mrs. Dang. Well, I'll try to endure their complaisance till you come.

[*Exit.*]

Ser. And Mr. Puff, sir, has sent word that the last rehearsal is to be this morning, and that he'll call on you presently.

Dang. That's true—I shall certainly be at home. — [*Exit* SERVANT.]—now, Sir Fretful, if you have a mind to have justice done you in the way of answer, egad, Mr. Puff's your man.

Sir Fret. Psha! sir, why should I wish to have it answered, when I tell you I am pleased at it?

Dang. True, I had forgot that. But I hope you are not fretted at what Mr. Sneer—

Sir Fret. Zounds! no, Mr. Dangle; don't I tell you these things never fret me in the least?

Dang. Nay, I only thought—

Sir Fret. And let me tell you, Mr. Dangle, 'tis damned affronting in you to suppose that I am hurt when I tell you I am not.

Sneer. But why so warm, Sir Fretful?

Sir Fret. Gad's life! Mr. Sneer, you are as absurd as Dangle: how often must I repeat it to you, that nothing can vex me but your supposing it possible for me to mind the damned nonsense you have been repeating to me! —let me tell you, if you continue to believe this, you must mean to insult me, gentlemen— and, then, your disrespect will affect me no more than the newspaper criticisms—and I shall treat it with exactly the same calm indifference and philosophic contempt— and so your servant.

[*Exit.*]

Sneer. Ha! ha! ha! poor Sir Fretful! Now will he go and vent his philosophy in anonymous abuse of all modern critics and authors. — But, Dangle, you must get your friend Puff to take me to the rehearsal of his tragedy.

Dang. I'll answer for't, he'll thank you for desiring it. But come and help me to judge of this musical family: they are recommended by people of consequence, I assure you.

Sneer. I am at your disposal the whole morning! —but I thought you had been a decided critic in music as well as in literature.

Dang. So I am—but I have a bad ear. I'faith, Sneer, though, I am afraid we were a little too severe on Sir Fretful— though he is my friend.

Sneer. Why, 'tis certain, that unnecessarily to mortify the vanity of any writer is a cruelty which mere dulness never can deserve; but where a base and personal malignity usurps the place of literary emulation, the aggressor deserves neither quarter nor pity.

Dang. That's true, egad! —though he's my friend!

SCENE II. —*A drawing-room in* DANGLE'S *House.*

MRS. DANGLE, SIGNOR PASTICCIO RITORNELLO, SIGNORE PASTICCIO RITORNELLO, INTERPRETER, *and* MUSICIANS *discovered.*

Interp. Je dis, madame, j'ai l'honneur to introduce et de vous demander votre protection pour le Signor Pasticcio Ritornello et pour sa charmante famille.

Signor Past. Ah! vosignoria, not vi preghiamo di favoritevi colla vostra protezione.

1 Signora Past. Vosignoria fatevi questi grazie.

2 Signora Past. Si, signora.

Interp. Madame—me interpret. —C'est a dire—in English— qu'ils vous prient de leur faire l'honneur—

Mrs. Dang. I say again, gentlemen, I don't understand a word you say.

Signor Past. Questo signore spieghero—

Interp. Oui—me interpret. —Nous avons les lettres de recommendation pour Monsieur Dangle de—

Mrs. Dang. Upon my word, sir, I don't understand you.

Signor Past. La Contessa Rondeau e nostra padrona.

3 Signora Past. Si, padre, et Miladi Fugue.

Interp. O! —me interpret. —Madame, ils disent—in English—Qu'ils ont l'honneur d'etre proteges de ces dames. —You understand?

Mrs. Dang. No, sir, —no understand!

Enter DANGLE *and* SNEER.

Interp. Ah, voici, Monsieur Dangle!

All Italians. Ah! Signor Dangle!

Mrs. Dang. Mr. Dangle, here are two very civil gentlemen trying to make themselves understood, and I don't know which is the interpreter.

Dang. Eh, bien!

[*The* INTERPRETER *and* SIGNOR PASTICCIO *here speak at the same time.*]

Interp. Monsieur Dangle, le grand bruit de vos talens pour la critique, et de votre interet avec messieurs les directeurs a tous les theatres—

Signor Past. Vosignoria siete si famoso par la vostra conoscenza, e vostra interessa colla le direttore da—

Dang. Egad, I think the interpreter is the hardest to be understood of the two!

Sneer. Why, I thought, Dangle, you had been an admirable linguist!

Dang. So I am, if they would not talk so damned fast.

Sneer. Well, I'll explain that—the less time we lose in bearing them the better—for that, I suppose, is what they are brought here for.

[*Speaks to* SIGNOR PASTICCIO—*they sing trios, &c.,* DANGLE *beating out of time.*]

Enter SERVANT *and whispers* DANGLE.

Dang. Show him up. —[*Exit* SERVANT.] Bravo!

admirable! bravissimo! admirablissimo! —Ah! Sneer! where will you find voices such as these in England?

Sneer. Not easily.

Dang. But Puff is coming. —Signor and little signoras obligatissimo! —Sposa Signora Danglena—Mrs. Dangle, shall I beg you to offer them some refreshments, and take their address in the next room.

[*Exit* MRS. DANGLE *with* SIGNOR PASTICCIO, SIGNORE PASTICCIO, MUSICIANS, *and* INTERPRETER, *ceremoniously.*]

Re-enter SERVANT.

Ser. Mr. Puff, sir. [*Exit.*]

Enter PUFF.

Dang. My dear Puff!

Puff. My dear Dangle, how is it with you?

Dang. Mr. Sneer, give me leave to introduce Mr. Puff to you.

Puff. Mr. Sneer is this? —Sir, he is a gentleman whom I have long panted for the honour of knowing—a gentleman whose critical talents and transcendent judgment—

Sneer. Dear Sir—

Dang. Nay, don't be modest, Sneer; my friend Puff only talks to you in the style of his profession.

Sneer. His profession.

Puff. Yes, sir; I make no secret of the trade I follow: among friends and brother authors, Dangle knows I love to be frank on the subject, and to advertise myself *viva voce*. — I am, sir, a practitioner in panegyric, or, to speak more plainly, a professor of the art of puffing, at your service—or anybody else's.

Sneer. Sir, you are very obliging! —I believe, Mr. Puff, I have often admired your talents in the daily prints.

Puff. Yes, sir, I flatter myself I do as much business in that way as any six of the fraternity in town. —Devilish hard work all the summer, friend Dangle, —never worked harder! But, hark'ee, —the winter managers were a little sore, I believe.

Dang. No; I believe they took it all in good part.

Puff. Ay! then that must have been affectation in them: for, egad, there were some of the attacks which there was no laughing at!

Sneer. Ay, the humorous ones. —But I should think, Mr. Puff, that authors would in general be able to do this sort of work for themselves.

Puff. Why, yes—but in a clumsy way. Besides, we look on that as an encroachment, and so take the opposite side. I dare say, now, you conceive half the very civil paragraphs and advertisements you see to be written by the parties concerned, or their friends? No such thing: nine out of ten manufactured by me in the way of business.

Sneer. Indeed!

Puff. Even the auctioneers now—the auctioneers, I say—though the rogues have lately got some credit for their language—not an article of the merit theirs: take them out of their pulpits, and they are as dull as catalogues! —No, sir; 'twas I first enriched their style—'twas I first taught them to crowd their advertisements with panegyrical superlatives, each epithet rising above the other, like the bidders in their own auction rooms! From me they learned to inlay their phraseology with variegated chips of exotic metaphor: by me too their inventive faculties were called forth: —yes, sir, by me they were instructed to clothe ideal walls with gratuitous fruits—to insinuate obsequious rivulets into visionary groves—to teach courteous shrubs to nod their approbation of the grateful soil; or on emergencies to raise upstart oaks, where there never had been an acorn; to create a delightful vicinage without the assistance of a neighbour; or fix the temple of Hygeia in the fens of Lincolnshire!

Dang. I am sure you hav done them infinite service; for now, when a gentleman is ruined, he parts with his house with some credit.

Sneer. Service! if they had any gratitude, they would erect a statue to him; they would figure him as a presiding Mercury, the god of traffic and fiction, with a hammer in his hand instead of a caduceus. —But pray, Mr. Puff, what first put you on exercising your talents in this way?

Puff. Egad, sir, sheer necessity! —the proper parent of an art so nearly allied to invention. You must know, Mr. Sneer, that from the first time I tried my hand at an advertisement, my success was such, that for some time after I led a most extraordinary life indeed!

Sneer. How, pray?

Puff. Sir, I supported myself two years entirely by my misfortunes.

Sneer. By your misfortunes!

Puff. Yes, sir, assisted by long sickness, and other occasional disorders: and a very comfortable living I had of it. *Sneer.* From sickness and misfortunes! You practised as a doctor and an attorney at once?

Puff. No, egad; both maladies and miseries were my own.

Sneer. Hey! what the plague!

Dang. 'Tis true, i'faith.

Puff. Hark'ee! —By advertisements—. Oh, I understand you.

Puff. And, in truth, I deserved what I got! for, I suppose never man went through such a series of calamities in the same space of time. Sir, I was five times made a bankrupt, and reduced from a state of affluence, by a train of unavoidable misfortunes: then, sir, though a very industrious tradesman, I was twice burned out, and lost my little all both times: I lived upon those fires a month. I soon after was confined by a most excruciating disorder, and lost the use of my limbs: that told very well; for I had the case strongly attested, and went about to collect the subscriptions myself.

Dang. Egad, I believe that was when you first called on me.

Puff. In November last? —O no; I was at that time a close prisoner in the Marshalsea, for a debt benevolently contracted to serve a friend. I was afterwards twice tapped for a dropsy, which declined into a very profitable consumption. I was then reduced to—O no—then, I became a widow with six helpless children, after having had eleven husbands pressed, and being left every time eight months gone with child, and without money to get me into an hospital!

Sneer. And you bore all with patience, I make no doubt?

Puff. Why yes; though I made some occasional attempts at *felo de se,* but as I did not find those rash actions answer, I left off killing myself very soon. Well, sir, at last, what with bankruptcies, fires, gout, dropsies, imprisonments, and other valuable calamities, having got together a pretty handsome sum, I determined to quit a business which had always gone rather against my conscience, and in a more liberal way still to indulge my talents for fiction and embellishment, through my favourite channels of diurnal communication—and so, sir, you have my history.

Sneer. Most obligingly communicative indeed! and your confession, if published, might certainly serve the cause of true charity, by rescuing the most useful channels of appeal to benevolence from the cant of imposition. But, surely, Mr. Puff, there is no great mystery in your present profession?

Puff. Mystery, sir! I will take upon me to say the matter was never scientifically treated nor reduced to rule before.

Sneer. Reduced to rule!

Puff. O Lud, sir, you are very ignorant, I am afraid! —Yes, sir,. puffing is of various sorts; the principal are, the puff direct, the puff preliminary, the puff collateral, the puff collusive, and the puff oblique, or puff by implication. These all assume, as circumstances require, the various forms of Letter to the Editor, Occasional Anecdote, Impartial Critique, Observation from Correspondent, or Advertisement from the Party.

Sneer. The puff direct, I can conceive—

Puff. O yes, that's simple enough! For instance, —a new comedy or farce is to be produced at one of the theatres (though by-the-by they don't bring out half what they ought to do)—the author, suppose Mr. Smatter, or Mr. Dapper, or any particular friend of mine—very, well; the day before it is to be performed, I write an account of the manner in which it was received; I have the plot from the author, and only add—"characters strongly drawn—highly coloured—hand of a master—fund of genuine humour—mine of invention—neat dialogue—Attic salt. " Then for the performance—"Mr. Dodd was astonishingly great in the character of Sir Harry. That universal and judicious actor, Mr. Palmer, perhaps never appeared to more advantage than in the colonel; —but it is not in the power of language to do justice to Mr. King: indeed he more than merited those repeated bursts of applause which he drew from a most brilliant and judicious audience. As to the scenery—the miraculous powers of Mr. De Loutherbourg's pencil are universally acknowledged. In short, we are at a loss which to admire most, the unrivalled genius of the author, the great attention and liberality of the managers, the wonderful abilities of the painter, or the incredible exertions of all the performers. "

Sneer. That's pretty well indeed, sir.

Puff. Oh, cool! —quite cool! —to what I sometimes do.

Sneer. And do you think there are any who are influenced by this?

Puff. O Lud, yes, sir! the number of those who undergo the fatigue of judging for themselves is very small indeed.

Sneer. Well, sir, the puff preliminary.

Puff. O, that, sir, does well in the form of a caution. In a matter of gallantry now—Sir Flimsy Gossamer wishes to be well with Lady Fanny Fete—he applies to me—I open trenches for him with a paragraph in the Morning Post. —"It is recommended to the beautiful and accomplished Lady F four stars F dash E to be on her guard against that dangerous character, Sir F dash G; who, however pleasing and insinuating his manners may be, is certainly not remarkable *for the constancy of his attachments!* " — in italics. Here, you see, Sir Flimsy Gossamer is introduced to the particular notice of Lady Fanny, who perhaps never thought of him before—she finds herself publicly cautioned to avoid him, which naturally makes her desirous of seeing him; the observation of their acquaintance causes a pretty kind of mutual embarrassment; this produces a sort of sympathy of interest, which if Sir Flimsy is unable to improve effectually, he at least gains the credit of having their names mentioned together, by a particular set, and in a particular way— which nine times out of ten is the full accomplishment of modern gallantry.

Dang. Egad, Sneer, you will be quite an adept in the business.

Puff. Now, Sir, the puff collateral is much used as an appendage to advertisements, and may take the form of anecdote, — "Yesterday, as the celebrated George Bonmot was sauntering down St. James's Street, he met the lively Lady Mary Myrtle coming out of the park: —'Good God, Lady Mary, I'm surprised to meet you in a white jacket, — for I expected never to have seen you, but in a full-trimmed uniform and a light horseman's cap! ' — 'Heavens, George, where could you have learned that? ' — 'Why, ' replied the wit, ' I just saw a print of you, in a new publication called the Camp Magazine; which, by-the-by, is a 'devilish clever thing, and is sold at No. 3, on the right hand of the way, two doors from the printing-office, the corner of Ivy Lane, Paternoster Row, price only one shilling. '" *Sneer*. Very ingenious indeed!

Puff. But the puff collusive is the newest of any; for it acts in the disguise of determined hostility. It is much used by bold booksellers and enterprising poets. —"An indignant correspondent observes, that the new poem called Beelsebub's Cotillon, or Proserpine's Fete Champetre, is one of the most unjustifiable performances he ever read. The severity with which certain characters are handled is quite shocking: and as there are many descriptions in it too warmly coloured for female delicacy, the shameful avidity with which this piece is bought by all people of fashion is a reproach on the taste of the times, and a disgrace to the delicacy of the age. " Here you see the two strongest inducements are held forth; first, that nobody ought to read it; and secondly, that everybody buys it: on the strength of which the publisher boldly prints the tenth edition, before he had sold ten of the first; and then establishes it by threatening himself with the pillory, or absolutely indicting himself for *scan. mag.*

Dang. Ha! ha! ha! —'gad, I know it is so.

Puff. As to the puff oblique, or puff by implication, it is too various and extensive to be illustrated by an instance: it attracts in titles and resumes in patents; it lurks in the limitation of a subscription, and invites in the assurance of crowd and incommodation at public places; it delights to draw forth concealed merit, with a most disinterested assiduity; and sometimes wears a countenance of smiling censure and tender reproach. It has a wonderful memory for parliamentary debates, and will often give the whole speech of a favoured member with the most flattering accuracy. But, above all, it is a great dealer in reports and suppositions. It has the earliest intelligence of intended preferments that will reflect honour on the patrons; and embryo promotions of modest gentlemen, who know nothing of the matter themselves. It can hint a ribbon for implied services in the air of a common report; and with the carelessness of a casual paragraph, suggest officers into commands, to which they have no pretension but their wishes. This, sir, is the last principal class of the art of puffing—an art which I hope you will now agree with me is of the highest dignity, yielding a tablature of benevolence and public spirit; befriending equally trade, gallantry, criticism, and politics: the applause of genius—the register of charity—the triumph of heroism—the self-defence of contractors—the fame of orators— and the gazette of ministers.

Sneer. Sir, I am completely a convert both to the importance and ingenuity of your profession; and now, sir, there is but one thing which can possibly increase my respect for you, and that is, your permitting me to be present this morning at the rehearsal of your new trage—

Puff. Hush, for heaven's sake! —*My* tragedy! —Egad, Dangle, I take this very ill: you know how apprehensive I am of being known to be the author.

Dang. I'faith I would not have told—but it's in the papers, and your name at length in the Morning Chronicle.

Puff. Ah! those damned editors never can keep a secret I —Well, Mr. Sneer, no doubt you will do me great honour—I shall be infinitely happy—highly flattered—Dang. I believe it must be near the time— shall we go together?

Puff. No; it will, not be yet this hour, for they are always late at that theatre: besides, I must meet you there, for I have some little matters here to send to the papers, and a few paragraphs to scribble before I go. —[*Looking at memorandums.*] Here is *A conscientious Baker, on the subject of the Army Bread; and a Detester of visible Brick-work, in favour of the new invented Stucco;* both in the style of Junius, and promised for to-morrow. The Thames navigation too is at a stand. Misomud or Anti-shoal must go to work again directly. —Here too are some political memorandums—I see; ay— *To take Paul Jones and get the Indiamen out of the Shannon— reinforce Byron—compel the Dutch to—*so! —I must do that in the evening papers, or reserve it for the Morning Herald; for I know that I have undertaken to-morrow, besides, to establish the unanimity of the fleet in the Public Advertiser, and to shoot Charles Fox I the Morning Post. —So, egad, I ha'n't a moment to lose.

Dang. Well, we'll meet in the Green Room.

[Exeunt severally.

ACT II.

SCENE I. — The Theatre before the Curtain.

Enter DANGLE, PUFF, and SNEER.

Puff: No, no, sir; what Shakspeare says of actors may be better applied to the purpose of plays; they ought to be the abstract and brief chronicles of the time. Therefore when history, and particularly the history of our own country, furnishes anything like a case in point, to the time in which an author writes, if he knows his own interest, he will take advantage of it; so, sir, I call my tragedy The Spanish Armada; and have laid the scene before Tilbury Fort.

Sneer. A most happy thought, certainly I Dang. Egad it was—I told you so. But, pray now, I don't understand how you have contrived to introduce any love into it.

Puff. Love! oh, nothing so easy! for it is a received point among poets, that where history gives you a good heroic outline for a play, you may fill up with a little love at your own discretion: in doing which, nine times out of ten, you only make up a deficiency in the private history of the times. Now, I rather think I have done this with some success.

Sneer. No scandal about Queen Elizabeth, I hope?

Puff. O Lud! no, no; —I only suppose the governor of Tilbury Fort's daughter to be in love with the son of the Spanish admiral.

Sneer. Oh, is that all!

Dang. Excellent, i'faith! I see at once. But won't this appear rather improbable?

Puff. To be sure it will—but what the plague! a play is not to show occurrences that happen every day, but things just so strange, that though they never did, they might happen.

Sneer. Certainly nothing is unnatural, that is not physically impossible.

Puff. Very true—and for that matter Don Ferolo Whiskerandos, for that's the lover's name, might have been over here in the train of the Spanish ambassador, or Tilburina, for that is the lady's name, might have been in love with him, from having heard his character, or seen his picture; or from knowing that he was the last man in the world she ought to be in love with—or for any other good female reason. —However; sir, the fact is, that though she is but a knight's daughter, egad! she is in love like any princess!

Dang. Poor young lady! I feel for her already! for I can conceive how great the conflict must be between her passion and her duty; her love for her country, and her love for Don Ferolo Whiskerandos!

Puff. Oh, amazing! —her poor susceptible heart is swayed to and fro by contending passions like—

Enter UNDER PROMPTER.

Und. Promp. Sir, the scene is set, and everything is ready to begin, if you please.

Puff. Egad, then we'll lose no time.

Und. Promp. Though, I believe, sir, you will find it very short, for all the performers have profited by the kind permission you granted them.

Puff. Hey! what?

Und. Promp. You know, sir, you gave them leave to cut out or omit whatever they found heavy or unnecessary to the plot, and I must own they have taken very liberal advantage of your indulgence.

Puff. Well, well. —They are in general very good judges, and I know I am luxuriant. —Now, Mr. Hopkins, as soon as you please.

Und. Promp. [*To the* Orchestra.] Gentlemen, will you play a few bars of something, just to—

Puff. Ay, that's right; for as we have the scenes and dresses, egad, we'll go to't, as if it was the first night's performance, —but you need

not mind stopping between the acts— [*Exit* UNDER PROMPTER. —
Orchestra *play—then the bellrings.*] Soh! stand clear; gentlemen. Now
you know there will be a cry of down! down! —Hats off! —Silence!
—Then up curtain, and let us see what our painters have done for us.
[*Curtain rises.*]

SCENE II. —*Tilbury Fort.*

"*Two* SENTINELS *discovered asleep.* "

Dang. Tilbury Fort! —very fine indeed!

Puff. Now, what do you think I open with?

Sneer. Faith, I can't guess—

Puff. A clock. —Hark! —[*Clock strikes.*] I open with a clock striking,
to beget an awful attention in the audience: it also marks the time,
which is four o'clock in the morning, and saves a description of the
rising sun, and a great deal about gilding the eastern hemisphere.

Pang. But pray, are the sentinels to be asleep?

Puff. Fast as watchmen.

Sneer. Isn't that odd though at such an alarming crisis?

Puff. To be sure it is, —but smaller things must give way to a striking
scene at the opening; that's a rule. And the case is, that two great
men are coming to this very spot to begin the piece; now it is not to
be supposed they would open their lips, if these fellows were
watching them; so, egad, I must either have sent them off their posts,
or set them asleep.

Sneer. Oh, that accounts for it. But tell us, who are these coming?

Puff. These are they—Sir Walter Raleigh, and Sir Christopher Hatton.
You'll know Sir Christopher by his turning out his toes—famous,
you know, for his dancing. I like to preserve all the little traits of
character. —Now attend.

"*Enter* SIR WALTER RALEIGH and SIR CHRISTOPHER HATTON.

Sir Christ. True, gallant Raleigh! "

Dang. What, they had been talking before?

Puff. O yes; all the way as they came along. —[To the actors.] I beg pardon, gentlemen, but these are particular friends of mine, whose remarks may be of great service to us. — [*To* SNEER *and* DANGLE.] Don't mind interrupting them whenever anything strikes you.

"*Sir Christ.*

True, gallant Raleigh
But oh, thou champion of thy country's fame,
There is a question which I yet must ask
A question which I never ask'd before—
What mean these mighty armaments?
This general muster? and this throng of chiefs?"

Sneer. Pray, Mr. Puff, how came Sir Christopher Hatton never to ask that question before?

Puff. What before the play began? -how the plague could he?

Dang. That's true, i'faith!

Puff. But you will hear what he thinks of the matter.

Sir Christ.

"Alas I my noble friend, when I behold
Yon tented plains in martial symmetry
Array'd; when I count o'er yon glittering lines
Of crested warriors, where the proud steeds' neigh,
And valour-breathing trumpet's shrill appeal,
Responsive vibrate on my listening ear;
When virgin majesty herself I view,
Like her protecting Pallas, veil'd in steel,
With graceful confidence exhort to arms!
When, briefly, all I hear or see bears stamp

Of martial vigilance and stern defence,
I cannot but surmise—forgive, my friend,
If the conjecture's rash—I cannot but
Surmise the state some danger apprehends!"

Sneer. A very cautious conjecture that.

Puff. Yes, that's his character; not to give an opinion but on secure grounds. —Now then.

Sir Walt. "O most accomplish'd Christopher! "—

Puff. He calls him by his Christian name, to show that they are on the most familiar terms.

Sir Walt. O most accomplish'd Christopher! I find Thy staunch sagacity still tracks the future, In the fresh print of the o'ertaken past."

Puff. Figurative!

Sir Walt. Thy fears are just.

Sir Christ. But where? whence? when? and what The danger is, — methinks I fain would learn.

Sir Walt. You know, my friend, scarce two revolving suns, And three revolving moons, have closed their course Since haughty Philip, in despite of peace, With hostile hand hath struck at England's trade.

Sir Christ. I know it well.

Sir Walt. Philip, you know, is proud Iberia's king!

Sir Christ. He is.

Sir Walt. His subjects in base bigotry And Catholic oppression held; - while we, You know, the Protestant persuasion hold.

Sir Christ. We do.

Sir Walt. You know, beside, his boasted armament, The famed Armada, by the Pope baptized, With purpose to invade these realms—

Sir Christ. Is sailed, Our last advices so report.

Sir Walt. While the Iberian admiral's chief hope, His darling son—

Sir Christ. Ferolo Whiskerandos hight—

Sir Walt. The same—by chance a prisoner hath been ta'en, And in this fort of Tilbury—

Sir Christ. Is now Confined—'tis true, and oft from yon tall turret's top I've mark'd the youthful Spaniard's haughty mien Unconquer'd, though in chains.

Sir Walt. You also know— Dang. Mr. Puff, as he knows all this, why does Sir Walter go on telling him?

Puff. But the audience are not supposed to know any-thing of the matter, are they? Sneer. True; but I think you manage ill: for there certainly appears no reason why Sir Walter should be so communicative.

Puff. 'Fore Gad, now, that is one of the most ungrateful observations I ever heard! —for the less inducement he has to tell all this, the more, I think, you ought to be obliged to him; for I am sure you'd know nothing of the matter without it.

Dang. That's very true, upon my word.

Puff. But you will find he was not going on.

"*Sir Christ.* Enough, enough—'tis plain—and I no more Am in amazement lost! "—

Puff. Here, now you see, Sir Christopher did not in fact ask any one question for his own information.

Sneer. No, indeed: his has been a most disinterested curiosity!

Dang. Really, I find that we are very much obliged to them both.

Puff. To be sure you are. Now then for the commander-in-chief, the Earl of Leicester, who, you know, was no favourite but of the queen's. —We left off—*in amazement lost!*

"*Sir Christ.* Am in amazement lost. But, see where noble Leicester comes supreme in honours and command.

Sir Walt. And yet, methinks, At such a time, so perilous, so fear'd, That staff might well become an abler grasp.

Sir Christ. And so, by Heaven! think I; but soft, he's here! "

Puff. Ay, they envy him!

Sneer. But who are these with him?

Puff. Oh! very valiant knights: one is the governor of the fort, the other the master of the horse. And now, I think, you shall hear some better language: I was obliged to be plain and intelligible in the first scene, because there was so much matter of fact in it; but now, i'faith, you have trope, figure, and metaphor, as plenty as noun-substantives.

"*Enter* EARL OF LEICESTER, GOVERNOR, MASTER OF THE HORSE, KNIGHTS, &c. *Leic.*

How's this, my friends! is't thus your new-fledged zeal,
And plumed valour moulds in roosted sloth?
Why dimly glimmers that heroic flame,
Whose reddening blaze, by patriot spirit fed,
Should be the beacon of a kindling realm?
Can the quick current of a patriot heart
Thus stagnate in a cold and weedy converse,
Or freeze in tideless inactivity?
No! rather let the fountain of your valour
Spring through each stream of enterprise,
Each petty channel of conducive daring,
Till the full torrent of your foaming wrath
O'erwhelm the flats of sunk hostility!"

Puff. There it is—followed up!

"*Sir Walt.*

No more!—the freshening breath of thy rebuke
Hath fill'd the swelling canvas of our souls!
And thus, though fate should cut the cable of
  [*All take hands.*]
Our topmost hopes, in friendship's closing line
We'll grapple with despair, and if we fall,
We'll fall in glory's wake!

Leic.

There spoke old England's genius!
Then, are we all resolved?

All.

We are—all resolved.

Leic.

To conquer—or be free?

All.

To conquer, or be free.

Leic.

All?

All.

All. "

Dang. Nem. con. egad!

Puff. O yes! —where they do agree on the stage, their

unanimity is wonderful!

"Leic.

Then let's embrace—and now—[*Kneels.* "

Sneer. What the plague, is he going to pray?

Puff. Yes; hush! —in great emergencies, there Is nothing like a prayer.

"Leic.

O mighty Mars! "

Dang. But why should he pray to Mars?

Puff. Hush!

"Leic.

  If in thy homage bred,
Each point of discipline I've still observed;
Nor but by due promotion, and the right
Of service, to the rank of major-general
Have risen; assist thy votary now!

Gov.

Yet do not rise—hear me! [*Kneels.*]

Mast.

And me! [*Kneels.*]

Knight.

And me! [*Kneels.*]

Sir Walt.

And me! [*Kneels.*]

Sir Christ.

And me! [*Kneels.*]"

Puff. *Now pray altogether.*

"All.

Behold thy votaries submissive beg, That thou wilt deign to grant them all they ask; Assist them to accomplish all their ends, And sanctify whatever means they use To gain them! " Sneer. A very orthodox quintetto!

Puff. Vastly well, gentlemen! —Is that well managed or not? Have you such a prayer as that on the stage? Sneer. Not exactly.

Leic. [To PUFF.] But, sir, you haven't settled how we are to get off here.

Puff. You could not go off kneeling, could you?

Sir Walt. [To PUFF.] O no, sir; impossible!

Puff. It would have a good effect i'faith, if you could

exeunt praying! —Yes, and would vary the established mode of springing off with a glance at the pit. Sneer. Oh, never mind, so as you get them off! —I'll answer for it, the audience won't care how.

Puff. Well, then, repeat the last line standing, and go off the old way. "All. And sanctify whatever means we use To gain them.

[Exeunt.]"

Dang. Bravo! a fine exit.

Sneer. Well, really, Mr. Puff—

Puff. Stay a moment!

"The *SENTINELS* get up.

1 Sent. All this shall to Lord Burleigh's ear.

2 Sent. 'Tis meet it should. [*Exeunt.*]"

Dang. Hey! —why, I thought those fellows had been asleep?

Puff. Only a pretence; there's the art of it: they were spies of Lord Burleigh's.

Sneer. But isn't it odd they never were taken notice of, not even by the commander-in-chief?

Puff. O Lud, sir! if people who want to listen, or overhear, were not always connived at in a tragedy, there would be no carrying on any plot in the world.

Dang. That's certain.

Puff. But take care, my dear Dangle! the morning gun is going to fire. [*Cannon fires.*]

Dang. Well, that will have a fine effect!

Puff. I think so, and helps to realize the scene. — [*Cannon twice.*] What the plague! three morning guns! There never is but one! —Ay, this is always the way at the theatre: give these fellows a good thing, and they never know when to have done with it. —You have no more cannon to fire?

Und. Promp. [*Within.*] No, sir.

Puff. Now, then, for soft music.

Sneer. Pray, what's that for?

Puff. It shows that Tilburina is coming! —nothing introduces you a heroine like soft music. Here she comes!

Dang. And her confidant, I suppose?

111

Puff. To be sure! Here they are—inconsolable to the minuet in Ariadne! [Soft music.]

"*Enter* TILNURINA *and* CONFIDANT.

Tilb.

Now has the whispering breath of gentle morn Bid Nature's voice and Nature's beauty rise; While orient Phoebus, with unborrow'd hues, Clothes the waked loveliness which all night slept In heavenly drapery I Darkness is fled. Now flowers unfold their beauties to the sun, And, blushing, kiss the beam he sends to wake them— The striped carnation, and the guarded rose, The vulgar wallflower, and smart gillyflower, The polyanthus mean—the dapper daisy, Sweet-William, and sweet marjoram—and all The tribe of single and of double pinks! Now, too, the feather'd warblers tune their notes Around, and charm the listening grove. The lark! The linnet! chaffinch! bullfinch! goldfinch! greenfinch! But O, to me no joy can they afford! Nor rose, nor wallflower, nor smart gillyflower, Nor polyanthus mean, nor dapper daisy, Nor William sweet, nor marjoram—nor lark, Linnet nor all the finches of the grove! "

Puff. Your white handkerchief, madam! —

Tilb. I thought, sir, I wasn't to use that till *heart-rending*

woe.

Puff. O yes, madam, at *the finches of the grove,* if you please.

"*Tilb.*

Nor lark,

Linnet, nor all the finches of the grove! [Weeps.]

Puff. Vastly well, madam! *Dang.* Vastly well, indeed!

"*Tilb.*

For, O, too sure, heart-rending woe is now The lot of wretched Tilburina! "

Dang. Oh! —it's too much.

Sneer. Oh! —it is indeed.

"*Con.*

Be comforted, sweet lady; for who knows, But Heaven has yet some milk-white day in store?

Tilb. Alas! my gentle Nora, Thy tender youth as yet hath never mourn'd Love's fatal dart. Else wouldst thou know, that when The soul is sunk in comfortless despair, It cannot taste of merriment. "

Dang. That's certain. "*Con.* But see where your stern father comes It is not meet that he should find you thus. "

Puff. Hey, what the plague! —what a cut is here! Why, what is become of the description of her first meeting with Don Whiskerandos—his gallant behaviour in the sea-fight—and the simile of the canary-bird?

Tilb. Indeed, sir, you'll find they will not be missed.

Puff. Very well, very well!

Tilb. [*To* CONFIDANT.] The cue, ma'am, if you please. "*Con.* It is not meet that he should find you thus.

Tilb. Thou counsel'st right; but 'tis no easy task For barefaced grief to wear a mask of joy.

Enter. GOVERNOR..

Gov. How's this! —in tears? —O Tilburina, shame! Is this a time for maudling tenderness, And Cupid's baby woes? —Hast thou not heard That haughty Spain's pope-consecrated fleet Advances to our shores, while England's fate, Like a clipp'd guinea, trembles in the scale?

Tilb. Then is the crisis of my fate at hand! I see the fleets approach—I see—"

Puff. Now, pray, gentlemen, mind. This is one of the most useful figures we tragedy writers have, by which a hero or heroine, in consideration of their being often obliged to overlook things that are on the stage, is allowed to hear and see a number of things that are not.

Sneer. Yes; a kind of poetical second-sight!

Puff. Yes. —Now then, madam.

"*Tilb.* I see their decks Are clear'd! —I see the signal made! The line is form'd! —a cable's length asunder! I see the frigates station'd in the rear; And now, I hear the thunder of the guns! I hear the victor's shouts—I also hear The vanquish'd groan! —and now 'tis smoke- and now I see the loose sails shiver in the wind! I see—I see—what soon you'll see—

Gov. Hold, daughter! peace! this love hath turn'd thy brain The Spanish fleet thou canst not see—because—It is not yet in sight! "

Dang. Egad, though, the governor seems to make no allowance for this poetical figure you talk of.

Puff. No, a plain matter-of-fact man; —that's his character.

"*Tilb.* But will you then refuse his offer?

Gov. I must—I will—I can—I ought—I do.

Tilb. Think what a noble price.

Gov. No more—you urge in vain.

Tilb. His liberty is all he asks. "

Sneer. All who asks, Mr. Puff? Who is—

Puff. Egad, sir, I can't tell! Here has been such cutting and slashing, I don't know where they have got to myself.

Tilb. Indeed, sir, you will find it will connect very

well. " — And your reward secure. "

Puff. Oh, if they hadn't been so devilish free with their

cutting here, you would have found that Don Whiskerandos has been tampering for his liberty, and has persuaded Tilburina to make this proposal to her father. And now, pray observe the conciseness with which the argument is conducted. Egad, the

pro and *con* goes as smart as hits in a fencing match. It is indeed a sort of small-sword-logic, which we have borrowed from the French.

"*Tilb.* A retreat in Spain!

Gov. Outlawry here!

Tilb. Your daughter's prayer!

Gov. Your father's oath!

Tilb. My lover!

Gov. My country!

Tilb. Tilburina!

Gov. England!

Tilb. A title!

Gov. Honour!

Tilb. A pension!

Gov. Conscience!

Tilb. A thousand pounds!

Gov. Ha! thou hast touch'd me nearly! "

Puff. There you see-she threw in *Tilburina.* Quick, parry Carte with *England*! Ha! thrust in tierce *a title*! —parried by *honour*. Ha! *a pension* over the arm! —put by by *conscience*. Then flankonade with *a thousand pounds*—and a palpable hit, egad!

"*Tilb.* Canst thou—Reject the suppliant, and the daughter too?

Gov. No more; I would not hear thee plead in vain: The father softens—but the governor Is fix'd! [*Exit.*]"

Dang. Ay, that antithesis of persons is a most established figure.

"*Tilb.* 'Tis well, —hence then, fond hopes, —fond passion hence; Duty, behold I am all over thine—

Whisk. [*Without.*] Where is my love—my—

Tilb. Ha!

Enter DON FEROLO WHISKERANDOS.

Whisk. My beauteous enemy! —"

Puff. O dear, ma'am, you must start a great deal more than that! Consider, you had just determined in favour of duty—when, in a moment, the sound of his voice revives your passion— overthrows your resolution—destroys your obedience. If you don't express all that in your start, you do nothing at all.

Tilb. Well, we'll try again.

Dang. Speaking from within has always a fine effect.

Sneer. Very.

"*Whisk.* My conquering Tilburina! How! is't thus We meet? why are thy looks averse? what means That falling tear—that frown of boding woe? Ha! now indeed I am a prisoner! Yes, now I feel the galling weight of these Disgraceful chains—which, cruel Tilburina! Thy doting captive gloried in before. —But thou art false, and Whiskerandos is undone!

Tilb. O no! how little dost thou know thy Tilburina!

Whisk. Art thou then true? —Begone cares, doubts, and fears, I make you all a present to the winds; And if the winds reject you—try the waves. "

Puff. The wind, you know, is the established receiver of all stolen sighs, and cast-off griefs and apprehensions.

"*Tilb.* Yet must we part! —stern duty seals our doom Though here I call yon conscious clouds to witness, Could I pursue the bias of my soul, All friends, all right of parents, I'd disclaim, And thou, my Whiskerandos, shouldst be father And mother, brother, cousin, uncle, aunt, And friend to me!

Whisk. Oh, matchless excellence! and must we part? Well, if—we must—we must—and in that case The less is said the better. "

Puff. Heyday! here's a cut! —What, are all the mutual protestations out?

Tilb. Now, pray, sir, don't interrupt us just here: you ruin our feelings.

Puff. Your feelings! —but, zounds, my feelings, ma'am!

Sneer. No, pray don't interrupt them.

"*Whisk.* One last embrace.

Tilb. Now, —farewell, for ever.

Whisk. For ever!

Tilb. Ay, for ever! [*Going.*]"

Puff. 'Sdeath and fury! —Gad's life! —sir! madam! if you go out without the parting look, you might as well dance out. Here, here!

Con. But pray, sir, how am I to get off here?

Puff. You! pshaw! what the devil signifies how you get off! edge away at the top, or where you will—[*Pushes the* CONFIDANT *off.*] Now, ma'am, you see—

Tilb. We understand you, sir. "Ay, for ever.

Both. Oh! [*Turning back, and exeunt. —Scene closes.*]"

Dang. Oh, charming!

Puff. Hey! —'tis pretty well, I believe: you see I don't attempt to strike out anything new—but I take it I improve on the established modes.

Sneer. You do, indeed! But pray is not Queen Elizabeth to appear?

Puff. No, not once—but she is to be talked of for ever; so that, egad, you'll think a hundred times that she is on the point of coming in.
Sneer. Hang it, I think it's a pity to keep her in the green-room all the night.

Puff. O no, that always has a fine effect—it keeps up expectation.

Dang. But are we not to have a battle?

Puff. Yes, yes, you will have a battle at last: but, egad, it's not to be by land, but by sea—and that is the only quite new thing in the piece.

Dang. What, Drake at the Armada, hey?

Puff. Yes, i'faith—fire-ships and all; then we shall end with the procession. Hey, that will do, I think?,

Sneer. No doubt on't.

Puff. Come, we must not lose time; so now for the under-plot.

Sneer. What the plague, have you another plot?

Puff. O Lord, yes; ever while you live have two plots to your tragedy. The grand point in managing them is only to let your under-plot have as little connection with your main-plot as possible. —I flatter myself nothing can be more distinct than mine; for as in my chief plot the characters are all great people, I have laid my under-plot in low life, and as the former is to end in deep distress, I make the other end as happy as a farce. —Now, Mr. Hopkins, as soon as you please.

Enter UNDER PROMPTER.

Under Promp. Sir, the carpenter says it is impossible you can go to the park scene yet.

Puff. The park scene! no! I mean the description scene here, in the wood.

Under Promp. Sir, the performers have cut it out.

Puff. Cut it out!

Under Promp. Yes, sir.

Puff. What! the whole account of Queen Elizabeth?

Under Promp. Yes, sir.

Puff. And the description of her horse and side-saddle?

Under Promp. Yes, sir.

Puff. So, so; this is very fine indeed! —Mr. Hopkins, how the plague could you suffer this?

Mr. Hop. [*Within.*] Sir, indeed the pruning-knife—

Puff. The pruning-knife—zounds! —the axe! Why, here has been such lopping and topping, I shan't have the bare trunk of my play left presently! —Very well, sir—the performers must do as they please; but, upon my soul, I'll print it every word.

Sneer. That I would, indeed.

Puff. Very well, sir; then we must go on. —Zounds! I would not have parted with the description of the horse! —Well, sir, go on. —Sir, it was one of the finest and most laboured things. — Very well, sir; let them go on. —There you had him and his accoutrements, from the bit to the crupper. —Very well, sir; we must go to the park scene.

Under Promp. Sir, there is the point: the carpenters say, that unless there is some business put in here before the drop, they sha'n't have time to clear away the fort, or sink Gravesend and the river.

Puff. So! this is a pretty dilemma, truly! —Gentlemen, you must excuse me—these fellows will never be ready, unless I go and look after them myself.

Sneer. O dear, sir, these little things will happen.

Puff. To cut out this scene! —but I'll print it—egad, I'll print it every word! [*Exeunt.*]

ACT III.

SCENE I. — *The Theatre, before the curtain.*

Enter PUFF, SNEER, *and* DANGLE.

Puff. Well, we are ready; now then for the justices.

[*Curtain rises.*]

"JUSTICES, CONSTABLES, &c., *discovered.* "

Sneer. This, I suppose, is a sort of senate scene.

Puff. To be sure; there has not been one yet.

Dang. It is the under-plot, isn't it?

Puff. Yes. —What, gentlemen, do you mean to go at once to the discovery scene?

Just. If you please, sir.

Puff. Oh, very well! —Hark'ee, I don't choose to say anything more; but, i'faith they have mangled my play in a most shocking manner.

Dang. It's a great pity!

Puff. Now, then, Mr. justice, if you please.

"*Just.* Are all the volunteers without?

Const. They are. Some ten in fetters, and some twenty drunk.

Just. Attends the youth, whose most opprobrious fame And clear convicted crimes have stamp'd him soldier?

Const. He waits your pleasure; eager to repay The best reprieve that sends him to the fields Of glory, there to raise his branded hand In honour's cause.

Just. 'Tis well—'tis justice arms him! Oh! may he now defend his country's laws With half the spirit he has broke them all! If 'tis your worship's pleasure, bid him enter.

Const. I fly, the herald of your will. [*Exit.*]"

Puff. Quick, sir.

Sneer. But, Mr. Puff, I think not only the justice, but the clown seems to talk in as high a style as the first hero among them.

Puff. Heaven forbid they should not in a free country! — Sir, I am not for making slavish distinctions, and giving all the fine language to the upper sort of people.

Dang. That's very noble in you, indeed.

"*Enter* JUSTICE'S LADY. "

Puff. Now, pray mark this scene. "*Lady* Forgive this interruption, good my love; But as I just now pass'd a prisoner youth, Whom rude hands hither lead, strange bodings seized My fluttering heart, and to myself I said, An' if our Tom had lived, he'd surely been This stripling's height!

Just. Ha! sure some powerful sympathy directs Us both—

Enter CONSTABLE *with* Son. What is thy name?

Son. My name is Tom Jenkins—*alias* have I none— Though orphan'd, and without a friend!

Just. Thy parents?

Son. My father dwelt in Rochester—and was, As I have heard—a fishmonger—no more. "

Puff. What, sir, do you leave out the account of your birth, parentage, and education?

Son They have settled it so, sir, here.

Puff. Oh! oh!

"*Lady.* How loudly nature whispers to my heart Had he no other name?

Son. I've seen a bill Of his sign'd Tomkins, creditor.

Just. This does indeed confirm each circumstance The gipsy told! — Prepare!

Son. I do.

Just. No orphan, nor without a friend art thou—I am thy father; here's thy mother; there Thy uncle—this thy first cousin, and those Are all your near relations!

Lady. O ecstasy of bliss!

Son. O most unlook'd for happiness!

Just. O wonderful event! [*They faint alternately in each other's arms.*]"

Puff. There, you see, relationship, like murder, will out. "*Just.* Now let's revive—else were this joy too much! But come—and we'll unfold the rest within; And thou, my boy, must needs want rest and food. Hence may each orphan hope, as chance directs, To find a father—where he least expects!

[*Exeunt.*]"

Puff. What do you think of that?

Dang. One of the finest discovery-scenes I ever saw! — Why, this under-plot would have made a tragedy itself.

Sneer. Ay! or a comedy either.

Puff. And keeps quite clear you see of the other.

"*Enter* SCENEMEN, *taking away the seats.* "

Puff. The scene remains, does it?

Sceneman. Yes, sir.

Puff. You are to leave one chair, you know. —But it is always awkward in a tragedy, to have your fellows coming in in your play-house liveries to remove things. —I wish that could be managed better. —So now for my mysterious yeoman.

"*Enter* BEEFEATER.

Beef. Perdition catch my soul, but I do love thee. "

Sneer. Haven't I heard that line before?

Puff. No, I fancy not. —Where, pray?

Dang. Yes, I think there is something like it in Othello.

Puff. Gad! now you put me in mind on't, I believe there is—but that's of no consequence; all that can be said is, that two people happened to hit upon the same thought—and Shakspeare made use of it first, that's all.

Sneer. Very true.

Puff. Now, sir, your soliloquy—but speak more to the pit, if you please—the soliloquy always to the pit, that's a rule. "*Beef.* Though hopeless love finds comfort in despair, It never can endure a rival's bliss! But soft—I am observed.

[*Exit.*]"

Dang. That's a very short soliloquy.

Puff. Yes—but it would have been a great deal longer if he had not been observed.

Sneer. A most sentimental Beefeater that, Mr. Puff!

Puff. Hark'ee—I would not have you be too sure that he is a Beefeater.

Sneer. What, a hero in disguise?

Puff. No matter—I only give you a hint. But now for my principal character. Here he comes—Lord Burleigh in person! Pray, gentlemen, step this way—softly—I only hope the Lord High Treasurer is perfect—if he is but perfect!

"*Enter* LORD BURLEIGH, *goes slowly to a chair, and sits.* "

Sneer. Mr. Puff!

Puff. Hush! —Vastly well, sir! vastly well! a most interesting gravity.

Dang. What, isn't he to speak at all?

Puff. Egad, I thought you'd ask me that! —Yes, it is a very likely thing—that a minister in his situation, with the whole affairs of the nation on his head, should have time to talk! —But hush! or you'll put him out.

Sneer. Put him out; how the plague can that be, if he's not going to say anything?

Puff. There's the reason! why, his part is to think; and how the plague do you imagine he can think if you keep talking?

Dang. That's very true, upon my word!

"LORD BURLEIGH *comes forward, shakes his head, and exit.* "

Sneer. He is very perfect indeed! Now, pray what did he mean by that?

Puff. You don't take it?

Sneer. No, I don't, upon my soul.

Puff. Why, by that shake of the head, he gave you to understand that even though they had more justice in their cause, and wisdom in their measures—yet, if there was not a greater spirit shown on the part of the people, the country would at last fall a sacrifice to the hostile ambition of the Spanish monarchy. *Sneer.* The devil! did he mean all that by shaking his head?

Puff. Every word of it—if he shook his head as I taught him.

Dang. Ah! there certainly is a vast deal to be done on the stage by dumb show and expressions of face; and a judicious author knows how much he may trust to it.

Sneer. Oh, here are some of our old acquaintance.

"*Enter* SIR CHRISTOPHER HATTON *and* SIR WALTER RALEIGH.

Sir Christ. My niece and your niece too! By Heaven! there's witchcraft in't. —He could not else Have gain'd their hearts. —But see where they approach Some horrid purpose lowering on their brows!

Sir Walt. Let us withdraw and mark them. [*They withdraw.*]"

Sneer. What is all this?

Puff. Ah! here has been more pruning! —but the fact is, these two young ladies are also in love with Don Whiskerandos. — Now, gentlemen, this scene goes entirely for what we call situation and stage effect, by which the greatest applause may be obtained, without the assistance of language, sentiment, or character: pray mark!

"*Enter the two* NIECES.

1st Niece. Ellena here! She is his scorn as much as I— that is Some comfort still! "

Puff. O dear, madam, you are not to say that to her face! —Aside, ma'am, aside. —The whole scene is to be aside.

"*1st Niece.* She is his scorn as much as I—that is Some comfort still. [*Aside.*]

2nd Niece. I know he prizes not Pollina's love; But Tilburina lords it o'er his heart. [*Aside.*]

1st Niece. But see the proud destroyer of my peace. Revenge is all the good I've left. [*Aside.*]

2nd Niece. He comes, the false disturber of my quiet. Now vengeance do thy worst. [*Aside.*]

Enter DON FEROLO WHISKERANDOS.

Whisk. O hateful liberty—if thus in vain I seek my Tilburina!

Both Nieces. And ever shalt!

SIR CHRISTOPHER HATTON *and* SIR WALTER RALEIGH *come forward.*

Sir Christ. and Sir Walt. Hold! we will avenge you.

Whisk. Hold *you*—or see your nieces bleed! [*The two* NIECES *draw their two daggers to strike*

WHISKERANDOS: *the two* UNCLES *at the instant, with their two swords drawn, catch their two* NIECES' *arms, and turn the points of their swords to* WHISKERANDOS, *who immediately draws two daggers, and holds them to the two* NIECES' *bosoms.*]"

Puff. There's situation for you! there's an heroic group! —You see the ladies can't stab Whiskerandos—he durst not strike them, for fear of their uncles—the uncles durst not kill him, because of their nieces. —I have them all at a dead lock! —for every one of them is afraid to let go first.

Sneer. Why, then they must stand there for ever!

Puff. So they would, if I hadn't a very fine contrivance for't. —Now mind—

"*Enter* BEEFEATER, *with his halbert.*

Beef. In the queen's name I charge you all to drop Your swords and daggers!

[*They drop their swords and daggers.* "]

Sneer. That is a contrivance indeed!

Puff. Ay—in the queen's name.

Sir Christ. Come, niece!

Sir Walt. Come, niece! [*Exeunt with the two* NIECES.]

Whisk. What's he, who bids us thus renounce our guard?

Beef. Thou must do more—renounce thy love!

Whisk. Thou liest—base Beefeater!

Beef. Ha! hell! the lie! By Heaven thou'st roused the lion in my heart! Off, yeoman's habit! —base disguise! off! off! [*Discovers himself by throwing off his upper dress, and appearing in a very fine waistcoat.*] Am I a Beefeater now? Or beams my crest as terrible as when In Biscay's Bay I took thy captive sloop? "

Puff. There, egad! he comes out to be the very captain of the privateer who had taken Whiskerandos prisoner—and was himself an old lover of Tilburina's.

Dang. Admirably managed, indeed!

Puff. Now, stand out of their way.

"*Whisk.* I thank thee, Fortune, that hast thus bestowed A weapon to chastise this insolent. [*Takes up one of the swords.*]

Beef. I take thy challenge, Spaniard, and I thank thee, Fortune, too! [*Takes up the other sword.*]"

Dang. That's excellently contrived! —It seems as if the two uncles had left their swords on purpose for them.

Puff. No, egad, they could not help leaving them.

"Whisk. Vengeance and Tilburina!

Beef. Exactly so—

[*They fight—and after the usual number of wounds given,* WHISKERANDOS *falls.*]

Whisk. O cursed parry! —that last thrust in tierce Was fatal. — Captain, thou hast fenced well! And Whiskerandos quits this bustling scene For all eter—

Beef. —nity—he would have added, but stern death Cut short his being, and the noun at once! "

Puff. Oh, my dear sir, you are too slow: now mind me. — Sir, shall I trouble you to die again?

"Whisk. And Whiskerandos quits this bustling scene For all eter—

Beef. —nity—he would have added, —"

Puff. No, sir—that's not it—once more, if you please.

Whisk. I wish, sir, you would practise this without me—I can't stay dying here all night.

Puff. Very well; we'll go over it by-and-by. —[*Exi* WHISKERANDOS.] I must humour these gentlemen!

"Beef. Farewell, brave Spaniard! and when next—"

Puff. Dear sir, you needn't speak that speech, as the body has walked off.

Beef. That's true, sir—then I'll join the fleet.

Puff. If you please. —[Exit BEEFEATER.] Now, who comes on?

"Enter GOVERNOR, *with his hair properly disordered.*

Gov. A hemisphere of evil planets reign! And every planet sheds contagious frenzy! My Spanish prisoner is slain! My daughter, Meeting the dead corse borne along, has gone Distract! [*A loud flourish of trumpets.*] But hark! I am summoned to the fort: Perhaps the fleets have met! amazing crisis! O Tilburina! from thy aged father's beard Thou'st pluck'd the few brown hairs which time had left! [Exit.]"

Sneer. Poor gentleman!

Puff. Yes—and no one to blame but his daughter!

Dang. And the planets—

Puff. True. —Now enter Tilburina!

Sneer. Egad, the business comes on quick here.

Puff. Yes, sir—now she comes in stark mad in white satin.

Sneer. Why in white satin?

Puff. O Lord, sir—when a heroine goes mad, she always goes into white satin. —Don't she, Dangle?

Dang. Always—it's a rule.

Puff. Yes—here it is—[*Looking at the book.*]

"Enter Tilburina stark mad in white satin, and her confidant stark mad in white linen. "

"Enter TILBURINA *and* CONFIDANT, *mad, according to custom.* "

Sneer. But, what the deuce! is the confidant to be mad too?

Puff. To be sure she is: the confidant is always to do whatever her mistress does; weep when she weeps, smile when she smiles, go mad when she goes mad. —Now, Madam Confidant—but keep your madness in the background, if you please.

"Tilb. The wind whistles—the moon rises—see, They have kill'd my squirrel in his cage: Is this a grasshopper? —Ha! no; it is my Whiskerandos—you shall not keep him—I know you have him in your pocket—An oyster may be cross'd in love! —who says A whale's a bird? —Ha! did you call, my love? —He's here! he's there! —He's everywhere! Ah me! he's nowhere! [*Exit.*]"

Puff. There, do you ever desire to see anybody madder than that?

Sneer. Never, while I live!

Puff. You observed how she mangled the metre?

Dang. Yes, —egad, it was the first thing made me suspect she was out of her senses!

Sneer. And pray what becomes of her?

Puff. She is gone to throw herself into the sea, to be sure—and that brings us at once to the scene of action, and so to my catastrophe— my sea-fight, I mean.

Sneer. What, you bring that in at last?

Puff. Yes, yes—you know my play is called *The Spanish Armada*; otherwise, egad, I have no occasion for the battle at all. —Now then for my magnificence! —my battle! —my noise! —and my procession! —You are all ready?

Und. Promp. [*Within.*] Yes, sir.

Puff. Is the Thames dressed?

"Enter THAMES *with two* ATTENDANTS. "

Thames. Here I am, sir.

Puff. Very well, indeed! —See, gentlemen, there's a river for you! — This is blending a little of the masque with my tragedy—a new fancy, you know—and very useful in my case; for as there must be a procession, I suppose Thames, and all his tributary rivers, to compliment Britannia with a fete in honour of the victory.

Sneer. But pray, who are these gentlemen in green with him?

Puff. Those? —those are his banks.

Sneer. His banks?

Puff. Yes, one crowned with alders, and the other with a villa! —you take the allusions? —But hey! what the plague! —you have got both your banks on one side. —Here, sir, come round. — Ever while you live, Thames, go between your banks. —[*Bell rings.*] There; so! now for't! —Stand aside, my dear friends! —Away, Thames!

[*Exit* THAMES *between his banks.*]

[*Flourish of drums, trumpets, cannon, &c., &'c. Scene changes to the sea— the fleets engage—the music plays—"Britons strike home. "—Spanish fleet destroyed by fire-ships, &c. —English fleet advances—music plays, "Rule Britannia. "—The procession of all the English rivers, and their tributaries, with their emblems, &c., begins with Handel's water music, ends with a chorus to the march in Judas' Maccabaeus. —During this scene,* PUFF *directs and applauds everything—then Puff.* Well, pretty well—but not quite perfect. So, ladies and gentlemen, if you please, we'll rehearse this piece again to-morrow.

[*Curtain drops.*]

Lightning Source UK Ltd.
Milton Keynes UK
UKHW041353131222
413860UK00001B/10